WORLD WAR II

WORLD WAR II

A Short History

by

HENRI MICHEL

translated by
Gilles Cremonesi

SAXON HOUSE

Saxon House
D. C. Heath Ltd.
Farnborough
Hampshire
England
translation © 1973 D. C. Heath Ltd.

All rights reserved. No parts of this publication may be reproduced, stored in a retrieval system, or transmitted in any form or by any means, electronic, mechanical, photocopying, recording, or otherwise, without the prior permission of the publishers.

Credits for photographs: all photographs reproduced by kind permission of The Imperial War Museum, except number 3 Topical Press, 12 Plant news, 15 Paul Brickhill.

Photoset and printed in Malta by St Paul's Press Ltd

First published in French as
La Seconde Guerre Mondiale
© 1971 Presses Universitaires de France

ISBN 0 347 00001 0
LOC No. 73-1505

Contents

	List of Illustrations	vii
	Introduction	xii
I	The Success of the Fascist States	1
II	The Axis Empires	14
III	The Strengths and Weaknesses of the Great Alliance	32
IV	The Allied Victory	45
V	The World at the End of the War	64
	Notes	80

Illustrations

1 German tanks parade before Brandenberg Gate.

2 The Japanese conquest in China. A tank unit advancing in Hunan.

3 October 1939. The Germans bomb Warsaw.

4 The German occupation of Norway. The *Prince Eugen* advancing down a fjord.

5 Germans occupy the debris-laden beach at Dunkirk after British and French have withdrawn.

6   The indiscriminate bombing of London. Firemen at work at Eastcheap.

7   The aftermath of the German bombardment of London. Air-raid damage looking down from St. Paul's, January 1941.

8   The Japanese conquest. Parachutists landing on the Dutch East Indies.

9   The desert campaign. Tanks lead an infantry attack.

10   The wireless becomes a propaganda tool. A German long-range photo of transmitters on the English coast near Dover.

11   Governments used propaganda to boost morale and strengthen resolve.

12   Propaganda was also used to discredit the enemy and weaken morale. A leaflet dropped on England early in the war.

13   The invasion of Soviet Russia. German photograph of a bombing raid on a Black Sea port.

14   The Resistance. A photograph of Russian guerillas plotting strategy, showing the typical features of the Resistance, limited equipment, no uniforms, high risk.

15   The Soviet counter-offensive. Anti-aircraft guns in the Russian winter.

16   Merchant shipping was vital to the Allied strategy. A North Sea convoy carrying supplies to Soviet Russia.

17   The Battle of the Atlantic. A British boat rescues survivors from a badly damaged German submarine.

18   Prisoners of war numbered in the millions. British prisoners marched off by Germans after the unsuccessful raid on Dieppe, August 1942.

19   A typical image of a P.O.W. camp, Stalag Luft 3 in Silesia.

20   The aftermath of the Warsaw uprising in November 1944. Most of Warsaw was destroyed.

21 One of the pre-fabricated harbours used in the Normandy landing to facilitate the unloading of over a million men, and supplies and ammunition.

22 Troops wade ashore from an amphibious craft at Normandy, June 1944.

23 U.S. bombers drop bombs in formation.

24 Vapour trails left by fighters in aerial combat as seen from the ground.

25 Press photo of Allied and Soviet troops joining up at Torgau, 25 April 1945, for the final assault on Berlin.

26 The war in the Pacific. Australian troops reconquer New Guinea from the Japanese.

27 The American Pacific Fleet riding at anchor.

28 The American landing at Iwo Jima, a vital step in the defeat of Japan.

29 The recapture of the Philippines. Amer-

icans engage Japanese ships off the Philippine coast.

30 The atom bomb. Photograph taken over Nagasaki just after the second atom bomb had been detonated over Japan.

31 The aftermath of the atom bomb. Photograph taken a half-mile from the centre of explosion looking away from the centre across the desolate remains of the city of Hiroshima.

Introduction

The Second World War has been regarded as a reaction or a sequel to the Great War of 1914–1918, but it was also profoundly different. More than any other, it upholds Gaston Bouthoul's theory that war is 'the most spectacular form of social violence ... marking a turning point in history'.

The Second World War was fought over a much vaster area than the First. Battles raged nearly everywhere in the world, on the glacial seas near Spitzbergen, in the heat of the Sahara, in the Alps, in the jungles of Burma, in Montevideo Harbour, in the Pacific atolls, on the banks of the Volga and of the Yellow River. For the first time in history social upheaval drew the whole of humanity into a single tragic struggle.

The Second World War also came nearer than the First to being a total war. Every country involved in the war, whatever its political and social system, made its best efforts to mobilise its entire population and economy. Not only were vast armies mustered – more than sixty million men were engaged in fighting – but all noncombatants, including women and young people, were liable to be called up to work in factories, arsenals or shipyards or to do other work of national importance. In America alone, the civilian work force totalled fifty million.

The war effort also mobilised ideas. Intensive propaganda campaigns were so effective in Germany and Japan as to maintain morale until the eve of surrender, while in occupied territories propaganda spurred the people to fight for liberation even after they had been disarmed. Even science was mobilised. There was no historical precedent for the combined effort in which scientists from all over the world assembled the first atomic bomb in the United States. The Second World War was both a military and a diplomatic conflict, but it was above all an economic and ideological conflict which raged on even in the Nazi concentration camps.

The world-wide character of this conflict, the vast improvements in armaments and the dogmas which whipped up fanaticism partially explain why the war was so immensely destructive. Aerial bombing was five times as effective by the end of the war as it had been five years earlier when the war began. The first atomic bomb detonated on 6 August 1945 was as powerful as 20,000 tons of ordinary explosives. Dresden burned and melted into the ground in a single night; Hiroshima in a few seconds. Millions of lives were lost in group executions, mass exterminations, and other hideous crimes which often had no bearing on the outcome of the war. The material and moral destruction, the lives and wealth lost were out of all proportion to the root causes which gave rise to the war.

Three separate theatres of war were fought over a six-year period. They were fought in parallel rather than in combination. As in the First World War, continental Europe assembled the largest armies and suffered the heaviest casualties, and was permanently and severely weakened as a result.

The Far East was another theatre of operations in the war. Fighting here was the first to begin and the last to end, and remained relatively isolated from fighting in Europe. The war in the Far East was of a different type, fought mainly by ships and aeroplanes working in close collaboration. Only the Americans and, to a lesser degree, the Russians fought in both theatres. This fact alone sheds light on the roles each of these nations played in the war.

The third war was a completely new phenomenon. The populations which had been temporarily conquered in Europe and China hit back at their new masters in an underground war. They fought regardless of conventional rules of combat with the assistance, or sometimes despite the presence, of professional soldiers.

The outcome of the war was unpredictable to the eleventh hour. Pitched battles were fought up to the last moments of the war. Even the composition of the two camps and the purposes for which they were fighting underwent dramatic reversals. Italy and Soviet Russia started as Germany's allies, or friendly neutrals, and became her enemies. France, who was the first to declare war on Germany, nearly wound up in the German camp.

War was originally declared to defend or restore the frontiers and the independence of Poland and China, but the English and Americans were eventually forced to jettison these goals in order to preserve their alliance with Soviet Russia. The ultimate paradox was America's attempt to dismantle the colonial empires of her allies, France and Britain, while assenting to political and social regimes in eastern and central Europe which were the antithesis of the ideals for which she had taken up arms.

Because of the widely divergent ideals for which the war was waged, it was bound to end ambiguously. No peace treaty was ever drafted. The defeated countries surrendered unconditionally as their conquerers demanded. This should have simplified problems. Other unforeseen problems cropped up requiring immediate and complex solutions, which some thought could only be found in a third world war between the Great Allies of the Second World War. Fortunately this did not come about, and measures were taken and organizations founded to insure against such a catastrophe.

It is a further paradox that after spending millions of lives in demolishing their enemies the victorious nations should work so diligently to rehabilitate them, and that their diligence should be so quickly rewarded.

The confused aftermath, however, must not obscure the importance of the war itself or its deep-seated causes. The two sides did not take up arms purely out of greed for spoils magnified into a programme of world domination. They were also fighting for the freedom of men and of nations, and in order to preserve their own ideals and values. The Second World War merits study not merely as an historical fact but because it produced a permanent twist in the evolution of human society and gave rise to grim speculations on the very nature of modern civilization. Our conclusions would have been very different if the outcome of the war had been different. And it might well have been.

Our account of the war thus follows the shape of the events themselves. At first the Axis Powers – Germany, Japan, and to a lesser degree Italy – enjoyed unbroken success, while their enemies lagged behind them in preparations for war and in their conception of it. This was the phase of the 'lightning war', which began in 1931 in Manchuria and finished at the end of 1942 on the banks of the Volga. By this time the aggressors had reached the limit of their resources in all theatres of operation, but their ambitions carried them beyond their means. Their advances were checked in several places at almost the same time, at Midway Island, at Stalingrad and at El Alamein, while counter-offensives began in Soviet Russia, in Libya and in French North Africa.

A world-wide war of attrition ensued. Both camps had large empires from which to draw resources. The winning side would not only have to amass the largest armies but also supply them with superior arms. The huge distance which had to be spanned in Soviet Russia and across the Pacific Ocean, combined with the almost limitless resources of the United States, tipped the balance in favour of the Allies. Their progress began slowly in 1943, accelerated during the summer of 1944 and reached a hurtling pace by the spring and summer of 1945. First Italy, then Germany and finally Japan were invaded, defeated and occupied. Each had to admit defeat and submit to the law of the conqueror.[1]

Whereas responsibility for starting the First World War appeared to be evenly distributed, initiatives were taken in Europe in September 1939, and in Asia in December 1941 unequivocally by one side and not the other. Hitler and the Japanese supreme command chose their time and their place and their enemies after careful preparation. A pre-war climate had prevailed for many years in Germany since the rise of Nazism, in Italy for much longer under the fascists, and in Japan after government had devolved on a group of military commanders. Each of the Axis Powers had compulsory savings programmes. Each had stockpiled arms and was making increased purchases of metals and chemicals. They had conscripted and equipped strong armies, navies and air forces. They had disciplined and indoctrinated their citizens and had fostered nationalistic sentiments. Detailed plans and strategies for winning a war had been drawn up.

It was not difficult to find reasons for going to war. The Germans felt strongly about their humiliating defeat in 1918 and the loss of territories under the Versailles Treaty. The Japanese and the Italians, who had been on the winning side in 1918, had no such pretext, and by September 1939 most of Germany's grievances had been settled. But propaganda in all three countries claimed that their territories could not sustain their populations, that they needed 'living space' to make up for the lack of colonial empires and to furnish food and raw materials. These claims appeared just to the Germans whose memory of the economic crises of the 1930's was still fresh, although living conditions had more or less returned to normal before the outbreak of war. In all three countries the parties which held, or seized, power aspired to colonizing imperialism.

Their ambitions were ill-defined and excessive and could only be satisfied at the expense of other, wealthier, powers. To justify them, the fascist parties claimed to have created the ideal form of government.

The future belonged to them, not to the decadent democracies which were condemned by their own imperfections. Germany and Japan boasted racial superiority.

These aims were published openly for the world to accept willy-nilly. The powers threatened by them could not amass the solid opposition necessary to obstruct them. For a period of several years, each responded in his own way. The United States were not in immediate danger and chose to remain impartial; the majority of Americans were committed to isolationism. The European states, on the other hand, especially those countries which had colonies, – could not afford to be impartial. But each of them gauged the danger differently and tried to evade it in its own way. Churchill and Eden saw the situation clearly, but the British government strove to maintain a balance in Europe, which seemed as likely to be toppled by French imperialism as by the German spirit of vengeance.

The French, who tirelessly championed the Versailles Treaty, could not shrug the German threat off, but under the Popular Front government France was divided by political and social crisis. The mass of the population hoped for higher living standards, which could only be achieved with continued peace, while some of the middle-ranking leaders were as much, or more concerned about the dangers of a popular revolution than by threats from across the border.

The smaller states, Poland and the Little Entente, which had been created out of the French victory in 1918, counted on a show of resistance by France to uphold their independence. Her hesitations and irresolution weakened their positions.

Soviet Russia was theoretically in the greatest danger. The Nazis had openly declared their intention to wipe out communism and to annex eastern Europe for 'living space'. Relations between the liberal democracies and the socialist democracies were governed by mutual suspicion and long-nourished mutual hostility which made the necessary cooperation impossible to achieve. Only tentative overtures were made between 1935 and 1939. Torn between unrealistic isolationism and the formation of a block, which insurmountable obstacles prevented, each tried to save his own skin in the hope that when a storm broke it would strike someone else. This was a short-sighted strategy which gave rise to a succession of appeasements and humiliations.

Mussolini, the first dictator, began the rule of force at home and conquest abroad. He had embarked on a policy of economic expansion in central Europe, threatening to dismember Yugoslavia and to avenge the defeat of the Italians at Adowa in 1895. His campaign to colonize Abyssinia in 1935 had seriously damaged the League of Nations, and after his victory in East Africa he revived territorial ambitions which brought the Italians into conflict with the French.

Japan pursued the same incautious policy on a larger scale in the Far East. Her economic conquest of China began after 1930. China was already submerged in civil war when the Japanese army invaded from Korea conquering Manchuria, and capturing a number of key cities, and gaining control of the main channels of communication.

But gravest provocation came from the victorious Nazis in Europe. A plebiscite restored the Saar to Germany. Then the left bank of the Rhine was remilitarized and Austria was annexed without drawing strong opposition. The settlement of the Sudeten question did arouse some opposition. France and Great Britain at first supported Czechoslovakia but later allowed her to be partitioned. In September 1938 at Munich, France and Britain signed a humiliating agreement from which Soviet Russia was excluded. Hitler's enemies were thus as disunited as they could possibly have been. There was no knowing whom he would choose as his next victim, but it was obvious that the 'policy of appeasement' had miscarried.

When Adolf Hitler absorbed Bohemia in March 1939, after having given his word not to do so, the British Prime Minister Neville Chamberlain was finally convinced that Hitler 'was not a gentleman'. Great Britain took the lead in forming an anti-German coalition, offering guarantees to all states threatened by Germans, even though she was in no position effectively to honour such guarantees.

Her approach to Soviet Russia for a political and military

treaty was perhaps too half-hearted to succeed, but it produced an unexpected result.

Stalin perceived the weakness of the Western democracies and did not wish to pay the cost of another Munich agreement. When Hitler made discreet soundings to find out whether Stalin was prepared to sign a non-aggression pact, Stalin quickly accepted. Perhaps he hoped to gain a breathing space for Soviet Russia. The real effect of the pact was to sign Poland's death warrant and to relieve Germany of any serious threat of a second front.

England and France felt that it would now be impossible for them to go back on their guarantee to support Poland. They declared war on Germany on 3 September 1939.

Europe's involvement in war left Japan free to act in the Far East. As the French and the British were already heavily engaged, Japan's real opponents were reduced to one – America. Colonial territories which could not be defended offered Japan the temptation of easy conquest. After shifting in several directions for nearly two years, the Japanese leaders resolved on a policy of expansion along the valuable shores of southeast Asia.

They had first to cancel out the possibility of interference from the the American fleet in the Pacific, and this they destroyed in its base at Pearl Harbour on 7 December 1941 without declaring war on America. The Nazis in Germany and the military clique in Japan thus brought war to Europe and Asia.

I The Success of the Fascist States

Fighting Forces at the Start of the War

In September 1939, the combined populations of Britain and France were much larger than Germany's. Their economic resources, their gold reserves and the potential resources of their empires were greater as well, although Germany had already swallowed up Austria and the Sudeten Germans. But the Reich was superior in active fighting forces, even if the Polish army was counted with the opposite camp and Italy was discounted because she had not yet declared war – she had declared herself 'non-belligerent', a new diplomatic category.

Although the Germans had a slight edge in submarines – they had 57 – the Royal Navy and the French fleet were unrivaled masters of the seas, and their position was strengthened by delays in the German navy's construction programme. Land forces were also fairly balanced. The British had only just revived compulsory military service and had only four divisions to send to France, but the French could assemble almost as many units as the Wehrmacht along their northern and eastern borders where the decisive battles seemed most likely to be fought, despite having to keep a number of units posted in Tunisia and in the Alps. France was further protected by the Maginot Line between the Rhine and Sedan.

The French army was still living off its victory in the First World War. It had won world renown, particularly in Germany, but it was not a modern army. Its leaders were old and stubbornly conservative.

Industrial resources were inadequate, and rearmament was further hampered by imprudent attempts to bolster the franc. As a result, although the French had as many tanks as the Germans, most of them were out of date. Moreover, the French command refused to concentrate them in armoured divisions as some of the more lucid officers, notably Colonel de Gaulle, had proposed. Only one 'armoured division' was created, and the rest of the tanks were dispersed among many divisions.

The two camps were especially unequal in air power. France and Britain had only 3,000 planes against the Luftwaffe's 4,000. Only a portion of the British air force was available for dispatch to France. The Royal Air Force had efficient fighter planes, but it was short of bombers, and the French had even fewer.

The German war machine was also subject to breakdown. The German population were orderly but unenthusiastic about taking up arms, despite their regimentation and Goebbels' propaganda. Germany had central Europe at her disposal, but she was critically short of iron and still shorter of petrol and rubber.

Italy's friendly neutrality and, more particularly, the pact with Soviet Russia probably gave Germany the chance to replenish stocks. But it would have been unwise for Germany to embark on a long war.

Hitler's strategy incorporated a clear-sighted understanding of these liabilities. First he would wipe out Poland. If France and Great Britain would not accept the accomplished fact, as he hoped, he would attack France before she had the chance to rearm. His plans were laid. The Wehrmacht would cross the Belgian plains as they had done in 1914.

French and British leaders knew how grimly deficient their armaments were. Although they had not yet set up an organization to oversee a unified war effort, they could rely on a fair degree of mutual understanding. They agreed to play for time in which to mobilize their full resources[2] and therefore remained on the defensive. Operations were confined to blockading Germany. A neutral block to frustrate German ambitions was assembled and an aerial offensive launched – of pamphlets. Bombing seemed too risky, since the Allies could not prevent Luftwaffe reprisals which might seriously impede French rearmament, and the Germans were within easy striking range of the main industrial regions of northern France and Lorraine.

This strategy was not inspired by solid determination. A number of English and a larger number of French leaders deplored the declaration of war, and hoped to avoid active fighting. The majority of Frenchmen, vividly remembering the slaughters of 1914–1918, recoiled from the prospect of renewing them. The English population generally, who occupied a less vulnerable position, presented a bolder front. The attitude which both countries first adopted towards the war undermined their willingness to fulfil their obligations towards Poland.

The Polish Campaign

Unlike her allies, Poland was set for a hard fight, although Polish leaders were sympathetic with the anti-Communist and anti-Semitic policies of the Nazis. But the Poles greatly overestimated their fighting strength. The generals expected to be able to resist an attack for several months, whereas their troops yielded within a few days to an overwhelming battering by the German Panzer divisions.

Poland fell on 18 September when the Red Army entered the fray. The government fled to Romania and the bulk of the Polish army was captured. Under a secret protocol in the Russo-German Pact, Poland was once again dissected by her larger neighbours. Soviet Russia permanently reappropriated those territories populated not by Poles but by Bielorussians and Ukrainians which had belonged to her under the Tsars. She also assumed authority over Lithuania. Germany annexed Danzig, Poznania and Upper Silesia and expelled their Polish communities. A nebulous state was allowed to survive around Cracow and Warsaw, called the 'General Government' by the Germans, which might later become 'Little Poland' and a vassal of the Reich for use as a bargaining point in future negotiations with the Allies.

The Allies, in fact, did not make the least attempt to rescue Poland. Britain ignored her solemn undertaking, and did not even consider the possibility of sending the Royal Navy into the Baltic. The French army marched a few miles into the Saar and then marched back. France and Great Britain seemed once again incapable of supporting an ally. Their failure to act proved that they were dangerously weak.

A more aggressive response might have been effective. The German generals, whose apprehensions were revealed later at the Nuremberg trials, had left only a sprinkling of troops to cover the west. These were inadequately protected by the half-complete Siegfried Line; the generals feared that such slight protection could easily break down. The French, who were in the middle of a heavy mobilization programme and had not the equipment for a break-through, failed to take advantage of a chance that would never recur.

The Phoney War

The eight months' lull in fighting which followed was called the 'phoney war'. It was no part of a German plan. Hitler ordered a westward attack several times, but each time it had to be postponed because of bad weather. The Allied armies remained poised for action. They had organized a huge joint operation. Great Britain used the extra time to equip a powerful expeditionary force, to arrange delivery of aeroplanes ordered from the United States, and to complete the field defences between the end of the Maginot Line and the sea. The long period of inactivity, however, undermined the Allied troops' morale. It encouraged the hope that Germany would not attack on the west but would rather turn against Soviet Russia.

During the winter of 1939–1940, a Soviet attack on Finland provoked a wave of anti-Soviet feeling in France, and the Allies discussed plans to rescue Finland. There was even a suggestion to send planes from Syria on a bombing raid against the oil wells in the Caucasus.

The inactivity troubled the most resolute leaders in England and France, including Churchill and Paul Reynaud, who had replaced Daladier as French prime minister in March 1940; but they could not find a way of attacking Germany. Aside from a frontal attack on the Siegfried line, the most direct route lay across Belgium. Belgium was neutral, however, and had declared her intention of remaining so.

Although the Belgians counted on Allied support against a German invasion, King Leopold rebuffed every suggestion of landing Allied troops. As the Allies were democratic countries who had declared war in order to preserve human rights, they could not violate Belgium's neutrality.

Their only alternative was to make peripheral attacks. They projected a Balkan expedition on the model of the Salonika expedition of the First World War, but the Balkan states refused to be drawn into the war, being certain that they would not be supported if they were. The Allies' only success was Turkey's half-hearted undertaking to oppose Italy.

Allied strategy therefore turned to Norway. Swedish iron, which was vital to the German war industry, was shipped out of Narvik during the winter when the Baltic Sea was iced over. If this iron supply line could be cut, German war potential would be permanently debilitated. The British and French prepared a joint expedition under British command, expecting the traditionally pro-British Norwegian government to acquiesce after going through the motions of a formal protest. But the plan leaked out, and the Germans, who had earmarked Norway as a base for air and submarine attacks on Britain, pre-empted the Allies' move. They invaded Denmark and Norway on 9 April. In Denmark they were completely successful; the Danish army surrendered and the government submitted. In Norway military resistance was more lively. What is more, despite the warm welcome shown by Quisling and his supporters, King Haakon could not be persuaded to yield to a German invasion. He fought on for as long as he could and then retired to England. The Allies were driven back from every landing point and only managed to capture Narvik.

The Battle of France

After 10 May, events in France forced a withdrawal from Narvik, but despite German successes, the Allies had not entirely wasted the interval of the 'phoney war'.

The French had used it to create three new tank divisions and were just forming a fourth. But the Germans had ten better equipped tank divisions at their disposal in Poland. These were grouped into armoured divisions which moved in orderly co-ordination with air and motorized infantry forces.

Although France and England by now had a larger number of modern planes, and the planes which they had purchased from America had begun to arrive, they were short of bombers, and instead of concentrating their air power into large strategic groupings as the Luftwaffe did, they dispersed them over several fronts. The Allied forces were about as large as the Wehrmacht, but they had a smaller number of active divisions. Although

German superiority was not crushing on paper, it became dramatically so as fighting began.

The German command also used the forced inactivity, from winter till summer 1940, to rejig their plans. Hitler replaced his modified version of the 1914 Schlieffen Plan with a daring scheme of von Manstein's in which the main thrust would be made across the Ardennes into a central point in the French defences. This plan caught the French completely unawares. Convinced that the Ardennes was impassable to tanks, they had guarded it with only a weak force made up largely of reserves. Ironically, their defences were concentrated on Belgium. The chiefs of staff had feared a face-to-face confrontation, for which the French army, they felt, was psychologically and politically unprepared. Since they could not allow the Belgian army to be wiped out, they decided to cross the frontier into Belgium as soon as possible after any German invasion.

Since the French would not have time to reach the Albert Canal at the eastern border of Belgium, they would meet the Belgian army half way. It was a hazardous scheme which was not adequately co-ordinated with the Belgians' plans.

Operations nevertheless began well. On the left flank the Seventh French Army gave valuable support to the Dutch, although the effort turned out to be fruitless and the Dutch surrendered after three days' fight. On 15 May, after the Anglo-French forces had advanced into Belgium and had more or less contained the German advance, they were cut off to the south and had to fall back.

Seven German armoured divisions had crossed the Ardennes in record time, against practically no resistance and, on 12 May, had reached the banks of the Meuse. Thereafter the Allied command was repeatedly outpaced, always a day or an idea too late. It was not until 15 May that they realized how serious the situation was, and by this time they did not have sufficient tanks or bombers to master it.

They sent their forces into battle in dribs and drabs which the Germans instantly wiped out. Guderian's tanks made a gigantic sweep of the sickle on 20 May, capturing Amiens and thrusting down towards Abbeville. The Belgian army, the British expeditionary force and the crack French units were trapped.

General Weygand, who replaced Gamelin as supreme commander of the Allied forces, drew up a plan which might reasonably have permitted the cornered troops to counter the enemy's pincer movement, a series of co-ordinated attacks from north and south allowing them to escape southwards. But defeat had already jeopardized the coalition. It was every man for himself.

The King of the Belgians surrendered without forewarning the Allies. The British commander ordered the British expeditionary force to retreat north to the coast and embark. By a tactical error, Hitler halted his tanks and gave about 330,000 troops the chance to withdraw from Dunkirk between 26 May and 4 June. All their heavy equipment, however, was left behind.

No active British forces were left in France; and practically none in England for that matter.

Now Weygand tried to form a continuous front across a narrower area along the Somme and the Aisne. Although the French soldiers fought hard, they could not withstand the Germans. Their front broke between 4 and 8 June, before the German tanks advancing from every direction. They reached the Atlantic and the Pyrenees and the Mediterranean, where they supported the Italians who had declared war on 10 June, after the battle was over. The French government fled to Bordeaux, and a tragic exodus of several million people followed. The French abandoned a plan for a 'retreat to Brittany'.

They rejected Churchill's proposal for a complete political unification with Great Britain, ruled out a retreat to North Africa, and decided to negotiate an armistice after Paul Reynaud was replaced by Marshal Pétain as head of the French government. The armistice was signed at Rethondes and at Rome, and took effect on 25 June. The German victory was ruthless and complete, and shocked the whole world.

Stalin warmly congratulated Hitler.

The Battle of Britain

Britain now stood alone. Opinion was not unanimously in favour of continuing the fight against such unlikely odds. Some leaders suggested that Lloyd George should negotiate a settlement with Hitler. But Churchill, the new prime minister, ignored the German overtures. The future of the free world hung on his determination. The old warrior relied on American support and on the resources of the Commonwealth to unify the British people. He galvanized them with his energy. Even so it was by no means certain that the British had the means to hold out. The Royal Navy was strong enough to prevent an enemy landing, although the Norwegian campaign had shown that the most powerful battleships were vulnerable to attack. But the Norwegian campaign had also strained the German navy, which admitted that it could not now support a landing. Hitler renounced plans for invasion while Goering braced himself to tip the balance with the Luftwaffe.

In the summer of 1940 a remarkable series of aerial battles began. Quite without precedent, this phase of the war came to be known as the Battle of Britain. Thanks to radar, a technical advance of which Britain then enjoyed a monopoly, and thanks to the superiority of the British fighter planes, the British were able to inflict heavy losses on the German air force. Much to everyone's surprise, the Germans were forced to abandon the strategy of destroying the Royal Air Force and its airfields, and turned to indiscriminate bombing of cities, especially London, in the vain hope of breaking British morale.

The War in Africa

Churchill, far from losing hope, decided to shift the war away from Britain to Africa. He despatched to Egypt what tanks the British army had left, and with them troops from New Zealand, Australia and India.

Heavy losses were inflicted on the Italian navy at Taranto and Genoa, while Commonwealth troops advanced on Eritrea and Abyssinia. Graziani's army, which Mussolini had imagined would march victoriously into Cairo, was driven back across the Libyan desert. The British advanced five hundred miles between the end of 1940 and the beginning of 1941, capturing 100,000 prisoners. The Italians had betrayed their weakness, at least in this sector.

In London, the British granted asylum to the kings and legitimate governments of Holland, Norway, Poland, Czechoslovakia and Belgium.

In addition, a handful of Frenchmen answered General de Gaulle's call on 18 June. Calling themselves the Free French they continued to fight in violation of the armistice.

Under the terms of this armistice the Vichy government had been set up as the legitimate government of France. Fleets from

Denmark, Norway, Holland, the Dutch East Indies, the Belgian Congo and Equatorial Africa also rallied round de Gaulle and made a significant contribution to British naval power.

The British pinned their greatest hopes, however, on American aid. They received this under the Lend-Lease Bill, one of the most important programmes of the whole war, which Roosevelt passed through Congress in March 1941. Under it, countries fighting for freedom would receive war materials against a promise of payment at the end of the war. The Americans themsevels formed convoys to escort materials across the Atlantic to the British Isles.

The Invasion of Russia

By the Spring of 1941 Great Britain had emerged from the threat of annihilation, but she had by no means gained the upper hand.

When Mussolini invaded Greece in October 1940, Britain was unable to man a Balkan front. A British expeditionary force landed on the Greek mainland, but it was not strong enough to save the Greeks. When it was withdrawn to Africa, however, it was powerful enough to halt an Axis offensive.

In April 1941 the Germans invaded Yugoslavia on the pretext that she had violated the 'Tripartite Pact', and then pressed on to relieve the Italians in Greece. The British were forced hastily to re-embark. A daring German parachute operation rooted them out of Crete. King George had no place to go but Cairo. Throughout the continent, the Germans expropriated what wealth and equipment they found. Belief in ultimate German victory induced many citizens in the occupied states, including the Vichy Government, to 'collaborate' with the Germans. The imbalance between the two camps may not have increased in Britain's disfavour, but they continued to be unevenly matched. England had not won the war. No one knew how or when she would. Prospects remained uncertain until 21 June 1941, when the Wehrmacht invaded Soviet Russia.

The attack caught the Soviet heads of state, especially Stalin, by surprise. They had been careful to adhere to the letter of the Russo-German Pact, while openly pursuing their own interests. At the same time, they had proceeded with territorial acquisition. They absorbed the Baltic states and Lithuania. They took part of Bessarabia and Bukovina from Rumania, and they occupied part of Finland. These manoeuvres displeased Hitler, who had not abandoned the great plan flaunted in *Mein Kampf* of following the path of the Teutonic Knights to colonize the vast plain inhabited by the Slavs, whom he regarded as inferiors. His plan also had the merit of annihilating the bolshevik heresy.

The huge European force which Hitler hurled into his crusade comprised Finns, Hungarians, Slovaks, Rumanians, and Italians as well as volunteer contingents raised from occupied countries, including a few thousand Frenchmen. There were 205 divisions of infantry and 30 armoured divisions which marshalled 4,000 tanks. These ground forces were supported by 3,000 aircraft. Three groups of armies were pointed at three targets – Leningrad, Moscow and the Ukraine, which offered rich supplies of wheat and iron. It remained to be seen whether these troops were sufficient to occupy and hold the vast expanse of Soviet Russia.

It appeared that they might be for the first six months. The Red Army was large but disquietingly weak and ill-prepared for modern warfare. Stalin's purges had decimated the high command. Tanks had not been organized in large units, while Soviet fighter planes were no faster than German bombers. Fortifications were also weak. The Wehrmacht advanced three hundred miles in eighteen days of fighting and by 2 September, Leningrad was within range of enemy fire. At Kiev, which fell on 25 September, 600,000 prisoners were taken. By 2 October Moscow was under attack.

The Russians yielded but they did not give way. They provided for future contingencies by dismantling and transporting hundreds of factories and thousands of workers up to and across the Urals. They brought in reinforcements from Siberia and reorganized their high command, placing Zhukov in charge of Moscow defences. By winter, Leningrad was under siege but it did not capitulate. The Germans were forced back from Moscow. This, their last attempt at lightning war, did not bring them victory. It had become a war of attrition and appeared likely to drag on. By spring 1942, German offensive forces were still stronger than the Russian, but their manoevres were restricted to objectives along the Volga and in the Caucasus. Again the Russians yielded, but they retreated inch by inch. They had learned how to wage war and they had new equipment. In addition, the German policy of systematic terror in the occupied

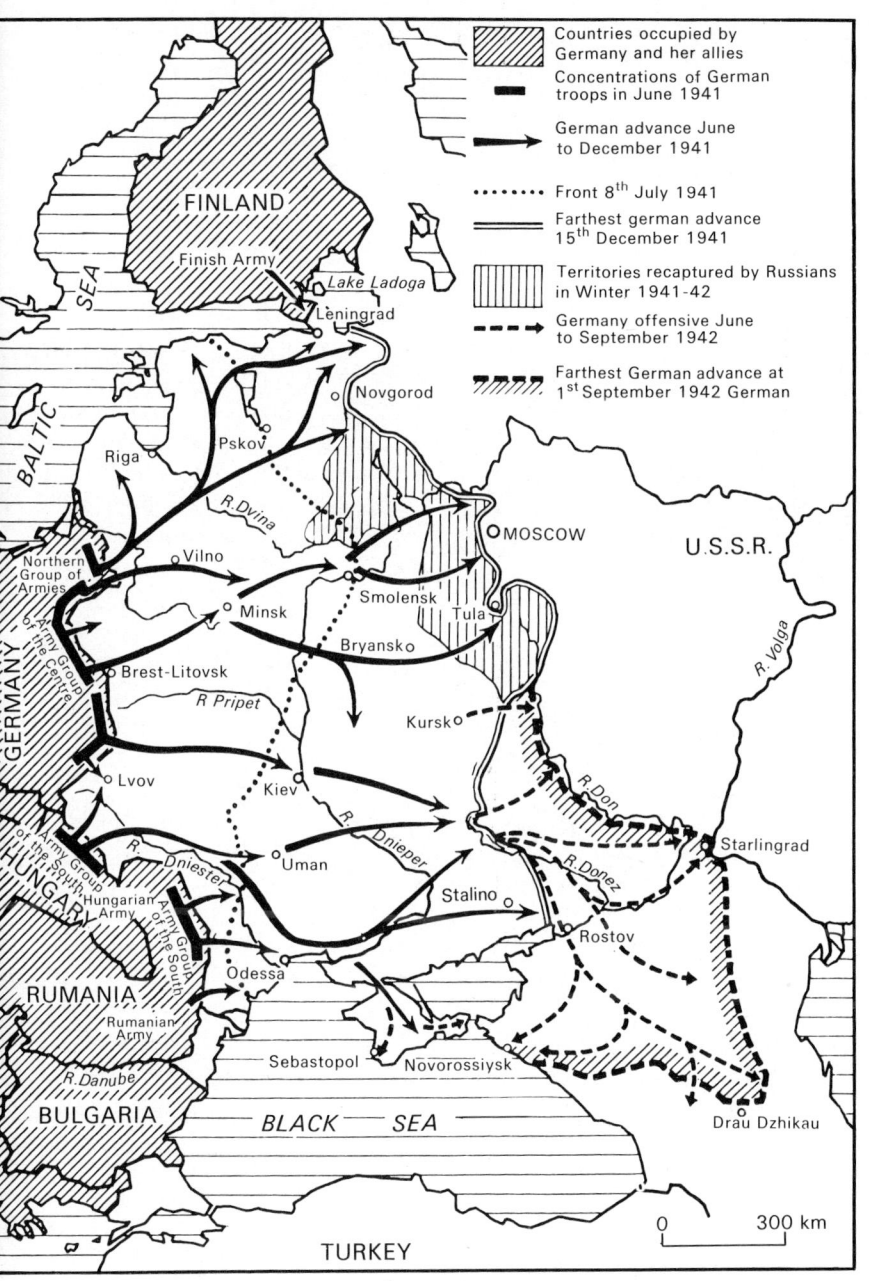

The German Invasion of Russia.

territories discouraged collaboration and prevented the formation of anti-Soviet splinter groups.

The Japanese Attack on Pearl Harbour and the Japanese Victories

The participation of a Eurasian power, Soviet Russia, gave the war a new dimension. The American-Japanese war made it a world war. After the fall of France, the Vichy government was forced to give the Japanese free access to Indochina. This enabled Japan to isolate China by blocking the road and the railway to Yunnan. The German invasion of Soviet Russia had surprised the Japanese command, but the Japanese declined a German invitation to invade Siberia. Instead they meticulously prepared a campaign to conquer South East Asia. They could not realize the plan without first preventing a counter-attack by the American fleet. On 7 December 1941 a daring air raid caught the American fleet riding at anchor several thousand miles away in Pearl Harbour. It was completely successful. The American fleet, except for three aircraft carriers, was disabled for months afterwards. Two days later, Japanese planes sank two powerful battle ships of the Royal Navy. The Asian seas became the private domain of the Japanese air and sea forces, and were to remain so for some time.

The United States had been caught by trickery. The previous controversy about American participation in the war was silenced and she entered the war with unhesitating resolution. Her industrial potential was immense, but a functioning war industry and a powerful army had still to be organized. The air force had scarcely been established and half the fighting fleet had been sunk.

The Japanese campaign was quick and thorough. In a few months, Hong Kong, the Philippines, the atolls in the central Pacific, the Dutch East Indies, Malaya and Singapore fell to Japan one after another. A peaceful entry into Siam was followed by the capture of Burma, the invaders winning the confidence of local nationalists by endorsing their agitation against European colonialism. India and Australia were threatened and troops had to be recalled from the Middle East to defend them.

The Pacific theatre of war covered an area incomparably greater than that of western Europe. Tokyo is over 4,000 miles from Hawaii, and Midway Island is 6,000 from Burma. The Japanese had to feed their troops and protect their convoys from American submarines, while consolidating their vast new empire and making it productive before the Americans could take the offensive. The Americans might then be discouraged from fighting back. It was not yet clear whether their naval forces, their air force, their merchant marine and their economy would be able to rise to the occasion.

Japanese and German victories placed their enemies in a precarious position between June 1941 and the spring of 1942. America, being new to submarine warfare, lost a catastrophic tonnage of shipping to the Germans in the Atlantic. It seemed that Germany, Italy and Japan might succeed in carving up the world as they had planned in September 1940 in their Tripartite Pact.

II The Axis Empires

The three Axis Powers ruled their conquered territories in roughly the same manner. They controlled government either directly or indirectly. They managed productive resources and manpower for their own profit. They diffused unrelenting propaganda and operated a watchful censorship. They suppressed civil liberties, recruited 'collaborators', and applied ruthless police action to silence the least opposition. They classified entire sectors of the population as enemies and annihilated them.

The Italian Empire

Italy was the least fortunate of the three winning countries. Mussolini was greedy. During the war itself he claimed operations in the Mediterranean basin as his private domain in which to direct his 'parallel war' as he thought fit. He reiterated his territorial claims at every possible opportunity. They included Nice, Corsica, Tunisia, Djibouti, the Sudan, part of Algeria, Epirus, Dalmatia. The Italians' weakness, however, was soon apparent. It seriously impaired the Duce's pretentions and undermined his authority. Italian troops managed to occupy a few slopes of the French Alps before 1942 and afterwards extended their domination to Corsica and the territory between the Rhone and the Alps. They held a few toeholds on the Dalmation coast and in British Somaliland. Croatia was theoretically an Italian dependency. But there was little profit in such meagre conquests.

Although the secret police, O.V.R.A., were brutal, the sympathies of the military chiefs were more royalist than fascist and they tended to be lenient. In Nice they even refused to enforce the Vichy government's anti-semitic laws. By 1943 Italy had lost everything – the empire which she had conquered before the war and all the territories she had won during the war.

The German Occupation of Europe

In the spring of 1942, German hegemony extended from the North Sea to Libya, from Finland to the Volga and the Caucasus. No such empire had ever dominated Europe. The haste with which states were annexed and Hitler's ulterior aims made the vast assemblage a hodgepodge of varying constitutional status. The regions which had previously belonged to the Reich were simply fused with it – Eupen and Malmédy, Luxembourg, Alsace-Lorraine (in violation of the Rethondes Armistice), a few Slovak provinces, Danzig, Pomerania, and Upper Silesia. For convenience Danish Sleswig was temporarily excluded.[3] It became illegal to use any language but German. German law was forcibly imposed. Troops were levied, and foreign elements in the population, such as the French-speaking citizens of Lorraine, were deported. Integration with Germany was completed by relocating populations. Entire villages in Alsace were transplanted across the Rhine.

Hitler declared these policies openly, but he took care not to disclose other plans. He seemed certain to reclaim the Reich's former colonies. From time to time he broadcast his interest in Atlantic 'bases', especially in Morocco on which both Spain and Italy also made claims. The 'Mediterranean Zone', which had become Italy's prerogative, remained imprecisely defined. Hitler did not explain how he would reunite colonies of German emigrants, '*the Volkdeutsche*', with their fatherland. The very notion of *Volkdeutsche* remained a hazy one. The Flemish, Norwegians, Dutch, Burgundians, and occasionally the Normans were considered *Volkdeutsche* in Nazi mythology.[4] Above all, he did not divulge his plans for central and eastern Europe. It was uncertain whether he would preserve a residual state of Poland, a sort of Grand Duchy of Warsaw, and whether he would carve Soviet Russia into large vassal states like the Ukraine.

In anticipation of victory, the Nazis drafted the conquered

states into their war effort as quickly as possible. Military governments were set up in the occupied sectors of Soviet Russia and throughout Western Europe, which was vulnerable to British attack. Norway and Holland were assigned German high commissioners. So was Bohemia, which was simply called a 'protectorate of the Reich'. Around the occupied states revolved satellite nations. They were German allies, ruled by dictators on a Nazi model, including Slovakia, Hungary, Rumania, Bulgaria, Serbia, and to a lesser extent, the Vichy government. Spain also belonged ideologically with the German block.[5] Sweden and Turkey were officially neutral but their economies were dominated by the Germans.

No part of Europe was immune to economic exploitation. At first property was requisitioned or pillaged. This continued throughout the war in Poland, Yugoslavia, and Soviet Russia, but subtler and more effective methods were eventually applied

The German War Effort

	1939	1940	1941	1942	1943	1944
Coal production (million tons)	332.8	364.8	402.8	407.8	429	432.8
Steel production (million tons)	22.5	21.5	31.8	32.1	34.6	28.5[a]
Petroleum products (million tons)		4,650	5,540	6,360	7,510	5,400[b]
German manpower (thousands)	39,100	34,800	33,100	31,300	30,300	29,000
German manpower in industry (thousands)	10,855	9,745	8,861	8,011	7,948	7,515
Foreign manpower in German economy (thousands)	300	1,150	3,020	4,120	6,260	7,130
Foreign manpower in industry (thousands)	104	236	644	1,001	2,061	2,367
Mobilized forces (thousands)	1,336	5,600	7,400	9,400	11,235	12,385
Production of guns		5,500	7,000	12,000	27,000	41,000
Production of tanks	2,000	2,200	5,120	9,395	19,885	27,300
Production of planes	8,296	10,247	12,400	15,409	24,807	37,950
Bombers only	2,886	3,952	4,350	6,537	8,589	6,468
Fighters only	1,856	3,146	3,744	5,215	11,738	28,925

[a]Production fell from 9.2 million tons in the first quarter to 3.9 in the last.
[b]Goering planned to produce 10 million tons in 1945; 1,000 tons were produced in February.

in western and central Europe. The mark became the European currency; its exchange rate was inflated to increase its buying power. The cost of maintaining the occupying forces was defrayed by the occupied states for their own 'defence'. These costs were incommensurate with the strength of the troops paid for.[6] This system assured unlimited credit to the German treasury, which, after 'corrections' were made, could practically buy the entire European economy. At the same time, trade 'agreements' were made and applied uniliterally.

Goods and materials were dispatched to Germany in exchange for promises of future rembursement. German economic policy gradually became clear. The Reich would retain political and economic control of Europe, where unification was a *leitmotiv* of German propaganda. Germany was to retain exclusive control of power through a monopoly on heavy industry and she magnified her prestige through a monopoly on culture. The other countries were cast in a colonial role as suppliers of raw materials and food. An immense colonization programme called 'Ostland' was undertaken before the war had ended. German colonies were installed in areas populated by Slavs, in Lorraine and in the Ardennes, in an effort to bolster and legitimize the German empire.

Greater Japanese Asia

When the Japanese wished to emphasize their victories they called their empire Greater Japanese Asia. When they wished to stress the collaboration of the 'liberated' populations, they called it the 'co-prosperity sphere'. It extended from Manchuria to Rangoon along the coast of East Asia and encompassed all of the archipelagos in the western Pacific as far as the western Aleutians and New Guinea. Its area in land and sea amounted to an eighth of the earth's surface. The Japanese believed they had a historic mission to fulfil. It was their task to prove that an Asiatic race was superior to the European races. They adapted European science and technology to their needs, but they preserved their own individuality. They would lead the colonized peoples on the path to liberation and progress. Before the war they had already made some attempt to rally emerging nationalism under the Japanese flag. After conquest they organized a Greater Asian Council and later a separate ministry – both steps toward direct rule or complete absorption.

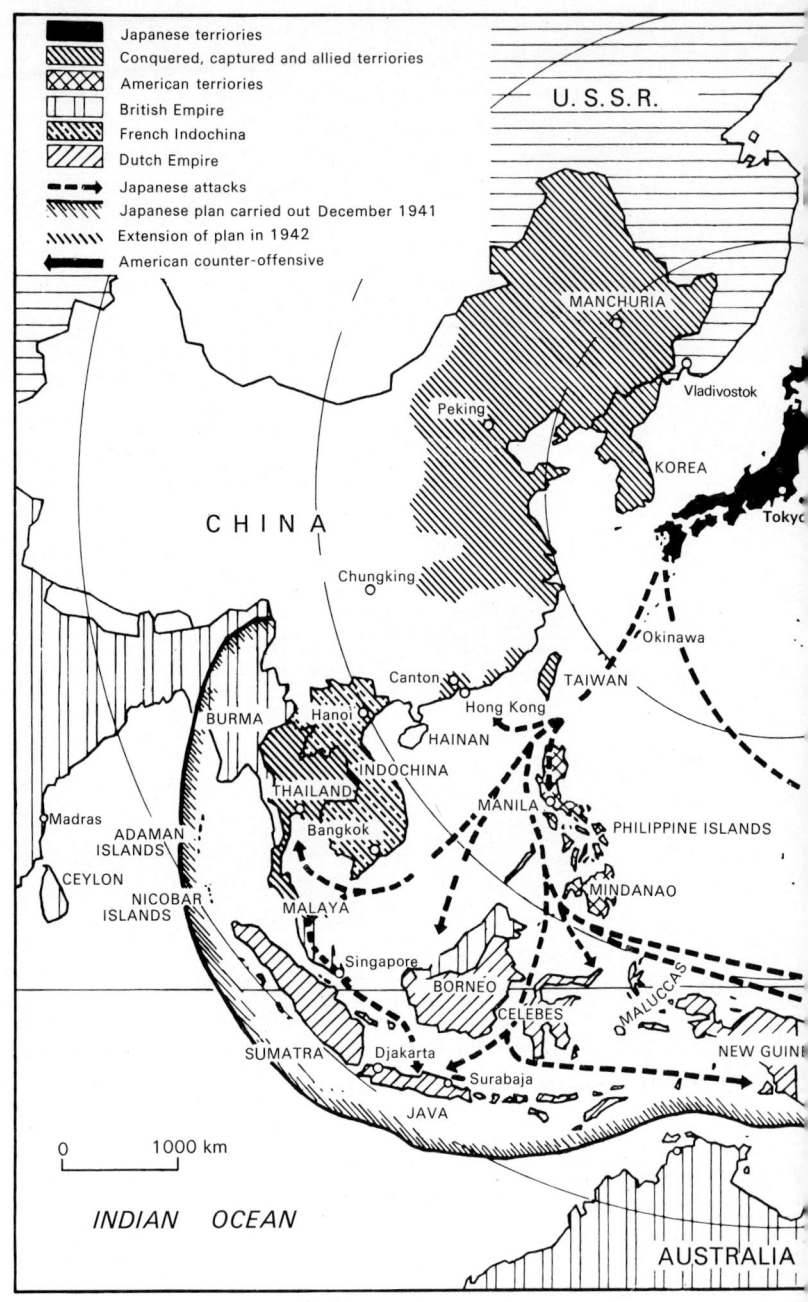

Greater Japanese Asia.

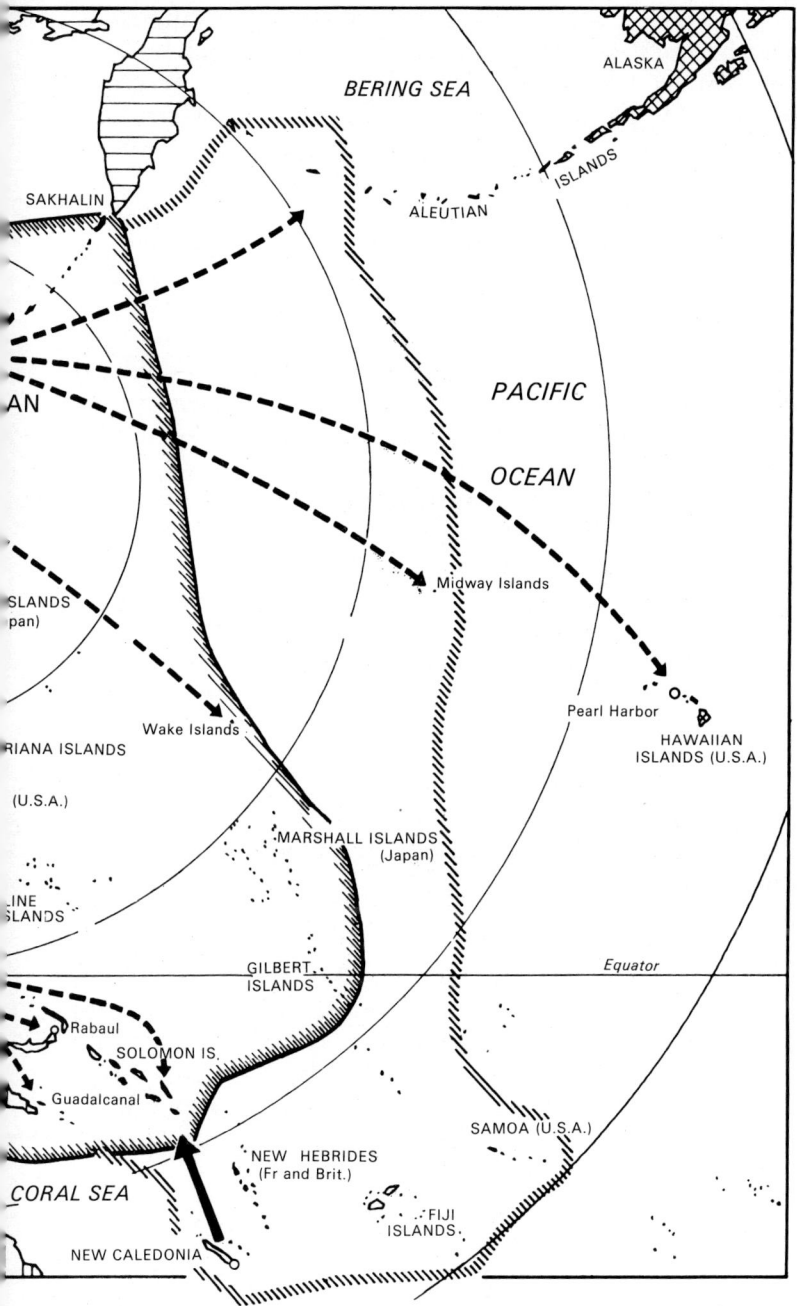

The Japanese were immediately trapped in the same contradiction as trapped the Germans. They needed both to protect their empire and to use it in the service of their war effort. It provided them with badly needed sources of energy and raw materials which would be vital to sustain a long war – coal, iron, petroleum, tin, rubber. The conquered territories were governed by military law. Since the navy remained separate from the army, however, and their respective commands guarded their autonomy jealously, it was difficult to administer a coordinated policy from Tokyo. The Japanese lacked time and capital and technical staff to develop the resources of their empire. They merely replaced the European colonial administrations as best they could in order to operate a policy of exploitation for their own greatest profit. A tinge of a superiority complex made them a little scornful of the populations they had 'liberated'.

The Japanese were strongly tempted to impose Japanese law, customs, language, commodities, even religion, on their empire. They often yielded to this temptation and emerged, in the eyes of the local elites, as merely another colonizer, no more beloved than their predecessors. The future of Greater Japanese Asia was as ill-defined as that of German Europe. One of the few certainties was that China was too big for Japan. A large part of China was simply inaccessible. The Japanese could not occupy China or subjugate it in its entirety. They won complete possession only of Manchuria, which became a satellite state with theoretical independence. Other countries were theoretically to be granted similar status: Burma and the Philippines in 1943, the Malaysian states and Indonesia at the end of the war. Borneo and New Guinea were to retain full colonial status.

The Japanese rewarded the loyalty shown by the Siamese with territory from Cambodia. For their own convenience they retained the French administration in Indochina until March 1945: an ambiguous European colonial rule continued. Japanese policy seems to have determined that India was not ripe for self-government, but India was beyond reach so long as the war continued.

The Collaborators

The conquerors claimed that they would make a 'new order' prevail in the occupied states. Some groups in these states motivated by ideology, others by opportunism, or by the expectation of profit declared their adherence to the new order. They were the 'collaborators'. Italy did not recruit many except from the substantial colonies of Italians in southern France and in Tunisia, whom the former consuls tried to organize. They failed completely in Corsica. A handful of Corsican adherents to the Italian 'new order' remained in Italy at a safe distance from their fellow-countrymen, who would have carved them to pieces.

The Nazis were more successful. They granted privileged status to the colonies of *Volkdeutsche* scattered about Hungary, Rumania, Slovakia and Croatia. People of German origin in these countries effectively enjoyed double nationality. They kept their language and appointed leaders who recognized Hitler as their Führer. They governed themselves and sometimes raised taxes for their own profit.

Nazi propaganda in the countries they occupied was cunning and persistent. Every medium was used to diffuse it, newspapers, books, films and especially the radio. Libraries were purged. Lecture series were organized, as well as concerts, exhibitions and performances of plays. Despite rivalry between departments in the German government, it was principally Goebbels' methods, which had been employed so successfully in Germany, which were adopted. Deviations from orthodoxy were silenced by a painstaking and fastidious censorship. The same propaganda slogans were repeated over and over again. Communists, they said, were pernicious. So were liberal democrats, freemasons and Jews. They condemned capitalists. They affirmed the superiority of fascist socialism, which was historically inevitable. They promised Europe peace and prosperity now that it had finally been unified by the German rod. These propaganda slogans were convincing so long as the Wehrmacht was winning battles. After the Wehrmacht stopped winning, propaganda was overshadowed by the facts themselves.

Groups of collaborators assembled in every state, except Poland and Soviet Russia where, despite separatist tendencies among minorities in these states, the Germans' systematic cruelty provoked unanimous opposition to the occupation. In most cases, 'collaborators' were drawn from fascist movements which had existed before the war, but their numbers swelled with new recruits. Some groups, such as the French Popular Party, transferred their allegiance to the Germans, while German subsidies created new groups. They modelled themselves on Nazism, aped Nazi rites and ceremonies, and furnished a supply of acolytes to staff the perverse operations of the German police. Although Quisling was given power in Norway, the Germans generally preferred to keep their collaborators in reserve, as a means of exerting pressure on the authorities in command. The Iron Guard in Rumania acted on Antonescu in this way. In France various groups in the occupied northern zone exerted pressure on the Vichy government. The groups of collaborators never accumulated a large following, except perhaps in Flanders and in Croatia. Public opinion generally ignored them or execrated them.

Japan made use of Japanese nationals who had already settled in the conquered countries as businessmen or industrialists. She also rallied the national liberation movements which had been encouraged by Japanese victory. In Nankin the Japanese set up a rival government to Chang Kai-Shek's. It planned to integrate China into the new Asia. In India they used Sadat Chandra Bose, a militant in the Congress Party, to foment an uprising. Unlike Nehru and Gandhi, Bose wanted to take advantage of British misfortunes of expell the British from India. The Japanese raised and outfitted a small volunteer army from Indian prisoners of war.

The Vichy Government

Many of the collaborators ironically claimed to be nationalists. Although some of them were sincere nationalists, they nevertheless accepted the rule of their conquerors. This contradiction was embodied most glaringly in the Vichy government. It was created by defeat and it capitalized on the discredit heaped on the Third Republic and the political parties which were held responsible for its failure. Marshal Pétain, head of the Vichy government, was immensely popular and he enjoyed almost unanimous support in the southern zone during the summer of 1940. After this good start two series of measures alienated popular support. He set up a new regime which he called the National Revolution. Its conception was heavily influenced by Charles Maurras, a political theorist who wrote for the journal *L'Action Française*. The National Revolution differed from fascism in a number of ways[7] but it was similar in others. Its first decision was to persecute categories of Frenchmen, including communists, socialists, Jews, freemasons. But its major defect was to be born under the occupation and to survive with German approval. The heads of the Vichy government were convinced that the German victory was irreversible. Their second mistake was a policy of systematic collaboration with the Germans. In the hope of mitigating German demands, they cashed in whatever stock France had saved in the Armistice. They negotiated the release of their prisoners of war. But Hitler reaped all they sowed without giving in return. Pétain opposed the reversal of alliances proposed by Pierre Laval, even though his own policy of collaboration helped the Germans without helping France. This policy was at variance with the progress of events. The Wehrmacht's set-backs eventually convinced the French that only the Allies could liberate them.

The Prisoners of War

The occupiers grew increasingly harsh as their needs and their setbacks mounted. They had progressively greater difficulty in winning over the occupied nations. Millions of prisoners or war had been taken in the 'lightning wars.' These languished in *oflags* and *stalags*. Because the Germans wanted to employ them as cheap manual labour, they freed only very few, and sometimes, as in the case of the Dutch prisoners, took them back. They used extreme measures to bring prisoners to heel. Because Soviet Russia had not signed the Geneva Convention the Germans felt free to deal the cruelest treatment out to Soviet prisoners.

The Terror of the SS

When military authorities were in complete control, they applied martial law firmly but reasonably. Captured opponents to their regime were tried as spies. Sometimes they were executed by firing-squads; more often they were imprisoned. The hostage system – the custom of punishing the innocent when the guilty parties could not be found – did much to further tarnish their image. But the military governments were mild compared with the SS, which gradually infiltrated everywhere.[8] Once the invasion of Soviet Russia was under way, the Wehrmacht was forced to hand over the SS responsibility for 'keeping order' behind the front lines.

In December 1941, Field-Marshal Keitel issued an enabling decree entitled 'Night and Fog', which authorized the SS to assume arbitrary powers. From that date, summary executions of communists, Jews and real or imagined enemies multiplied.

The SS also carried out group massacres, razings of whole villages, pitiless deportations of populations.

Their systematic reign of terror was introduced into western Europe in 1943. Persons suspected of committing acts of violence against the occupying forces were tortured.

Concentration Camps

The concentration camps, which were run by the SS, were typically Nazi institutions. Originally set up for Germans hostile to the regime, theoretically in order to reindoctrinate them, in practice they prevented opponents of Nazism for causing trouble.

On the outbreak of war the camps spread, to become international cities, in which tens of thousands of involuntary inhabitants lived in isolation from the world with their own social hierarchy and their own economy.

These camps were death factories. Thirteen large camps received detainees from the thousands of local units through which the SS organized their activities. The camps, perhaps, exemplified the 'new order', which the Nazis planned to impose on the world after victory. They claimed millions of victims.

Some of them, especially the Auschwitz-Birkenau complex, were reserved for Jews. Nazi hatred of the Jews was unquenchable. German propaganda taxed the Jews with every conceivable physical, moral and intellectual defect. It illogically held them responsible for capitalism, democracy and bolshevism. Jews had to be eradicated from society like a pestilence which would otherwise bring about the disintegration of nations. They were called the 'anti-race'. The Nazis used this metaphysical condemnation as grounds for humiliating them, secluding them from society, and depriving them of property under a policy of 'Aryanization of commerce'. The Jews were herded into ghettos in east Europe and sent to special camps for mass extermination. Six million perished in this way.[9]

The Underground Resistance[10]

People in occupied territories set up clandestine resistance movements against their conquerors.

These movements cropped up in every occupied country, without exception. Despite differences in their essential characters, they everywhere evolved in a similar way. Everywhere the oppressed boosted their morale by denigrating their conquerors. Avid for news, they listened eagerly to radio broadcasts from Allied stations – from Boston, Moscow, and, principally, the B.B.C. transmission from London. With the news pep-talks were broadcast and, later, instructions for action.

News was printed first in occasional pamphlets, then in news-sheets published as the opportunity arose.

Groups sprang up spontaneously and often survived and grew strong. They did what was within their means, improving their methods with experience. The German war machine was damaged by progressively more frequent and more effective sabotage operations.

Help was offered people pursued by the enemy, escaped prisoners of war, Jews, Allied pilots who had been shot down. A network of escape routes extended from Belgium to the Pyrenees and from Poland to Hungary and Greece. Air and sea operations landed and collected agents. Resistance groups gathered information useful to the Allied armies. The braver resistance fighters acquired skill by attacking 'collaborators' or isolated soldiers. Gradually, dissenting groups found hiding places in forests, especially after large numbers of young men were inducted into compulsory labour forces in Germany. Partisans and resistance fighters operated in combat units. The aims of the resistance were realized in the mass insurrections, repeated strikes, demonstrations, armed uprisings in cities, such as Paris and Warsaw, and in inadequately protected regions, such as Vercors and Slovakia, leading up to the Allied liberation.[11]

The Allies and the Resistance

Sometimes the clandestine resistance movements managed to capture enemy weapons. After the Italians surrendered, the Yugoslav partisans acquired the Italian occupying forces' equipment. But the resistance more often depended on the Allies to supply arms.

Career soldiers in every country remained sceptical about the 'little war'. The British, especially Churchill, appreciated its importance. They created a Special Operations Executive (S.O.E.) to supply equipment. Each of the exiled governments which had been granted asylum in London, including the French National Committee, looked after its own nationals. The news that the Free French Movement had defended Bir-Hakeim against Rommel's Afrika Korps did much to buoy the spirits of the Resistance in occupied French.

On the other hand, the British confined their sponsorship of the clandestine war to harassment of the enemy in multiple engagements. Although the Americans organized a nub of resistance against the Japanese in the Philippines, and after 1943 they provided most of the equipment for the European resistance, they found it difficult to adapt to resistance methods of warfare. Since the Red Army and the partisans were fighting side-by-side on home ground, they could be organized under a single command. Soviet Russia could also rely on support in every country; the communist parties were loyal to Russia and had a great deal more experience in clandestine operations than most of their fellow citizens. A number of national communist chiefs, notably Thorez from France and Togliatti from Italy, spent the entire war in Russia. Allied policies towards the resistance were identical in one respect. They supported resistance movements when to do so favoured their own interests. When it did not, they fought against them.

The Resistance in Western Europe

The resistance in Western Europe was equipped and organized by the British. Norway lay outside the sphere of large-scale military operations, but an underground resistance was founded and directed by military personnel. It undertook sabotage operations, of which the most spectacular was the destruction of the German 'heavy water' factory. The Danish resistance remained largely inactive until 1943, after which it organized strikes, but the whole of the population of Denmark remained loyal to the legitimate government. In Holland the resistance operated a vast relief system for victims of the occupation. It created an intelligence network which the Abwehr, the special intelligence and counter-espionage service in the Wehrmacht, failed for a long time to detect. The Belgians organized an escape network similar to that of the First World War. They also executed espionage and sabotage operations.

In France the underground movement was more complex. France had been divided into Zones of different status, while general disenchantment with the political parties of the Third Republic encouraged the formation of new groups. The resistance movements which grew with the help of a large underground press, generally became progressively more unified and more active. The first 'services' were set up through the efforts of Jean Moulin, and included news agencies, parachute drops, secret armies, and social welfare and educational programmes. These 'movements' combined with the labour unions and the reemerging political parties to form the National Council of Resistance. The Council adopted General de Gaulle's leadership, first from London and later from Algiers. By the time the Vichy government collapsed at the end of the war the resistance had effectively established a French government. It directed a full-scale clandestine resistance movement and consolidated traditional streams of public opinion. It also mustered a full-scale internal army, the French Forces of the Interior, which hid out in the '*maquis*' while preparing to liberate the nation and to reform its institutions and its economic structures.[12]

The Resistance in Central and Eastern Europe

In central and eastern Europe the resistance was more immediately and more resolutely committed to direct action, but it was also disabled by internal conflict which sometimes verged on civil war. During the first year of the war, while Soviet Russia was enduring almost continuous defeat, large units were separated from the main army but were not captured. The government and institutions of the Soviet regime were swept away. Dispersed troups had to be reformed and the Communist Party restored. After this band of several thousand partisans attacked behind the immense German front. They manoeuvred in areas which were too vast for thorough-going occupation. Their role was to cut the German supply lines, which had been overstretched, and to divert a large number of German divisions from the principal front, while the Red Army was preparing a counter-offensive. These operations were undertaken in an atmosphere of patriotic exultation. They marked the fulfilment of the Bolshevik regime's integration with traditional Russia.

President Benes of Czechoslovakia skilfully preserved national unity, by reaching an agreement with Soviet Russia outside and with the communists inside his country. The Slovak insurrection in summer 1944 was to be a great triumph in the European resistance movements.[13]

National unity could not be achieved in Poland, Yugoslavia or Greece, where the exiled governments and their partisans at home quarrelled with the communist partisan groups. In Poland, the memory of the Russo-German Pact and the Russian and German occupation which followed it drained the Poles' pro-Russian sympathies, especially those who had joined the government in exile. Efforts at a reconciliation bogged down when the corpses of several thousand Polish officers were discovered at Katyn. Thereafter Stalin gave support exclusively to the communist partisans. In August 1944 he even allowed the Germans to crush the Warsaw uprising. Tito, the leader of the partisans in Yugoslavia, was underpinned by the English, not the Russians. He fought against the Croat and Serbian collaborators and the 'Četnici' resistance of Mihailovič, as well as the occupying forces. The partisans readiness to fight gave them an edge. Their struggle moulded Yugoslavia after the war. As in Soviet Russia, Yugoslav resistance operations constituted a separate front. In Greece communists fought constantly and bitterly with anti-communists. The British wished to assure their control of the Mediterranean and intervened against the communists, whom Stalin, by an agreement with Churchill, allowed the British to crush.

While the Axis powers were at war, opposition to the regime was regarded as high treason. This policy produced moral conflicts which paralysed the exiled Germans for a long time. Although the opposition inside Germany had largely been herded into concentration camps, some sabotage work was accomplished and information was collected on behalf of the Russians. On 20 July 1944, however, when defeat was imminent, a handful of German military chiefs tried to assassinate Hitler and to seize power. They failed and paid for their desperate attempt with their lives.

Anti-fascist emigration from Italy was larger and more resolute, but it was fragmented. As Italian defeats mounted, the anti-fascists returned and the various factions sensibly joined forces. But Mussolini was finally toppled without their intervention. The formation of the Liberation Committees after Mussolini's fall gave them a more active role to play. In reconquered Italy, they tried to persuade the Allies to turn their backs on King Victor Emanuel, whom they held responsible for fascism. In the parts of Italy under German occupation, the Committees organized partisan groups. They fought in the same conditions as the French and Yugoslav partisans and sometimes linked operations with them.

The Resistance in China

The heaviest resistance fighting occurred in China under the leadership of Mao Tse-Tung, who sometimes cooperated with the official government of Chiang Kai-Shek and sometimes fought against him. Mao Tse-Tung managed to organize a basic programme of guerilla warfare fought over a wide, relatively remote area and to integrate this programme into the formation of a new political, cultural and social system in China. Unlike Russian bolshevism, Chinese communism convassed recruits from the peasant masses, from small property holders and from agricultural labourers. The need for concerted action against a common foreign enemy was emphasized during the war. Land was not confiscated; even capitalist industrialists were enlisted. Simultaneously the cadres were prepared for a revolution which would follow liberation on the basis of a coalescence of party, army and people. Banks, land, factories and large businesses would be socialized. The endless struggle, Mao Tse-Tung said, would be fought on three planes – political, economic and cultural; revolution would continue long after bourgeois structures had been dismantled. The principles of Chinese communism, although inspired by Lenin, thus diverged from Russian communism.

The Chinese example and the Japanese victories gave stimulus to national movements among the colonized peoples. Their wakening enevitably occurred at the expense of those Allies who had colonial empires – Great Britain, France and Holland. It was boosted by Roosevelt's anti-colonial policy, which conflicted with Churchill's on this point, as much as by Soviet propaganda and by the communist parties. Great Britain, however, was fighting to liberate states dominated by Nazi imperialism, while France and Holland were fighting for their own freedom. They each found it difficult to ignore national aspirations in their colonies. Yet Churchill refused to become 'the gravedigger of the British Empire'. He refused to promise India her independence, and suppressed dissident activities in Iraq and Egypt.[14]

Japanese policies in Asia alienated some nationalist movements – notably in the Philippines and in Burma. The Chinese communities in the Indian archipelago and Malaya were centres of opposition to Japanese domination. In Indochina, the Viet Minh tried to play the new colonizers off against the old. Japanese policy in Indonesia sought to oppose both the traditional muslim population and youthful reformers. Despite conflicts and misunderstandings, however, the majority of people in most of these countries remained sympathetic to movements which opposed European colonization. Before evacuating these territories, the Japanese armies handed their arms and powers over to the nationalists, thereby effectively ruling out the return of European colonizers, particularly in Indonesia and Indochina.

The alternate defeats of the armies in North Africa discredited both camps and encouraged the Arabs to revolt. The French government at Algiers promised and was forced actually to grant independence to Syria and Lebanon during the war. The Algerian nationalists did not stir while the Vichy government was in power, but the American landing roused them to action. The French provisional government promised huge reforms. The resistance in France disliked the prospect of losing French territories. The Vichy government was blamed and the resistance fell into the position of having simultaneously to fight both their enemies and the Allies in order to keep France intact. General de Gaulle had announced to the Blacks in Brazzaville, who had rarely rebelled in the past, that they would have greater autonomy but not independence. Ironically, the Arab nationalists in Iraq and North Africa cooperated with Nazi Germany although a German military victory would have brought German ideology and a much more rigid domination than under European rule. Whatever the methods and means, colonized peoples everywhere had begun to revolt. In Latin America, as well, separation from Europe and increased dependency on the United States produced mounting hostility towards the 'Yankees'.

The Importance of the Resistance

It is difficult to measure how much the resistance contributed to the war effort, least of all quantitatively. The number of men employed, or the number of battles fought, do not provide any real index of its importance. Taken as a whole the resistance movement constituted an auxiliary force. It was the Great Allies themselves who won the war; resistance movements would have withered away without them. Even in Soviet Russia it is clear that the resistance played a secondary role compared with that of the Red Army. Nevertheless the contribution made by the resistance even in a military sphere was appreciable. In an age of machine warfare, it demonstrated that more time-worn methods stood a chance of success. The most important and the most lasting effects of resistance activity were felt on a political level. After the war some states, such as Norway, Holland, and Belgium, returned to a situation which had existed before the war, but others such as France and Italy were totally transformed, as if a revolution had occurred. Soviet Russia and the communists gained most. The courage which they had shown in battle completely overshadowed the Russo-German Pact. In many places they installed themselves permanently in power. The establishment of the people's democracies in eastern and central Europe began in national insurrections which, in turn, originated in the underground resistance. On an ideological plane, they demonstrated that some of Lenin's teachings were still relavant. Political transformation, however, was most radical outside Europe, especially in China. Although the decisions taken by the Allied Powers helped to shape the world after the war, the struggles for freedom in the occupied states contributed a vast amount in determining political and economic systems as much as popular attitudes.

III The Strengths and Weaknesses of the Great Alliance

Great Britain, Soviet Russia and the United States were thrown into alliance by German and Japanese attacks. By combining resources and coordinating military operations they could amass overwhelming forces, but immense obstacles needed to be overcome. Their deeply opposed ideologies and mentalities bred mutual distrust. Each of them needed to mobilize her entire economy and to manufacture more and better arms than the enemy, who had prepared longer and had already won immense advantages. They needed to formulate goals which did not conflict with a coordinated strategy. Although Germany and Japan benefited from unified commands and efficient internal lines of communication, each conducted her own war without joining forces, and without reaching a common understanding. The Allies, on the other hand, had to face all the problems inherent in coalitions, and their cooperation had to span vast distances. Before examining how they launched the great offensive which won them the war, it is worth looking at the programme upon which their success was founded.

The Turning Point of the War

Throughout 1941 and 1942 the Allies remained on the defensive, waiting for the enemy offensive to flag. Towards the end of 1942 a change of tide occurred on all fronts. The Allies had not yet assembled their full resources, but the enemy was showing signs of strain. This was the turning point in the war.

The change began in the Pacific. The Japanese had never planned to invade America or to draw America into an all-out war, but merely to compel the Americans to recognize their Asian Empire. In April 1942, planes from an American aircraft carrier, which had escaped destruction at Pearl Harbour, bombed Tokyo. The Japanese were deeply shaken and decided to broaden their 'defensive perimeter' to include the Aleutian Islands and Hawaii. They sent a large fleet to capture Midway Island, but the Americans, who had deciphered the Japanese code, were able to prepare a defence. The Japanese were badly defeated on 4 and 5 June 1942, largely by American air superiority. The Japanese lost four aircraft carriers, and with them the air and naval advantage won at Pearl Harbour. A little later, in August 1942, the Americans launched their first amphibious landing and checked the Japanese southward advance at Guadalcanal. All Japanese supplies had to be transported by sea, and their lines of communication were overstretched. Their convoys were vulnerable and succumbed easily to American submarine attacks. The Japanese had lost a million tons of ships by the end of December 1942. Although the Americans had not launched a counter-offensive in the Pacific, they had succeeded in halting Japanese expansion.

The Italo-German forces in Africa also met with reverses. While the Soviet offensive was underway Hitler could not spare large forces to make inroads towards Gibraltar, Malta and Bizerta in the Mediterranean. He sent a few squadrons of Luftwaffe to Sicily and an army, under the command of Rommel, to Libya. Both camps received essential supplies from convoys, which were constantly subject to attack. The Allied convoys sailed east and west across the Mediterreanean while the Axis convoys sailed north and south. Malta was in a key position at the crossroads of the two shipping lanes. In spring 1942, after Rommel's request for reinforcements had been granted, he launched an offensive which arrived within forty miles of Alexandria in a single leap. The British fleet cautiously evacuated the port of Alexandria. Egypt was threatened and Egyptian nationalists began to stir. Mussolini prepared to march triumphantly into Cairo on a white charger. But Rommel, who had spent some of his forces and had extended supply lines for his offensive, did not have enough petrol and tanks left for the last thrust to victory. At the same time, American equipment reached the British. They appointed a new commander for their forces, and drew up meticulous plans for a counter-attack, which Montgomery launched at El Alemein at the end of October 1942. The attack succeeded and by January 1943 he had captured Tripoli.

The Americans landed in Morocco and Algeria on 8 December 1942 in the Allies' first large scale counter-offensive, which caught the Axis forces from behind. The French troops in Africa defied the Vichy government's orders to oppose the Allies and helped to make the landing a success despite the Allied generals' inexperience. But the success was limited. From a military point of view, the line of attack was too narrow to prevent the Italo-German army forming bridgeheads at Tunis and at Bizerta to rescue the Afrika Korps. Admiral Darlan's unexpected arrival at Algiers precipitated an epidemic of political intrigue. Although Darlan had been chosen to succeed Pétain in the Vichy government, the Americans elevated him to civil and military head of the government at Algiers against the objections of both the Free French movement and the resistance. Darlan's assassination in December 1942 did not settle the matter. After the Germans invaded the southern zone of France and the French fleet was scuttled at Toulon, the Vichy government effectively withdrew from France, but revived in the Allied camp at Algiers. The advantages gained by the Allied landing, however, were incontestable. Malta was saved. The Afrika Korps had merely been granted a stay of execution. The fragile length of Italy was now fully exposed to Allied invasion.

The British could not have achieved this break-through on their own. They had become increasingly dependent on American consignments of men and arms. The delivery of these in Anglo-American convoys across the Atlantic to the British Isles was seriously hampered by attacks of German submarines.

Between September 1939 and December 1941 the Germans sank 8 million tons of Allied merchant shipping. Losses were still heavier in June 1942: 800,000 tons were sunk. Every four hours an Allied ship sank with all hands. British shipyards worked uninterruptedly while American shipyards proliferated along the shores of the Great Lakes. Their combined output, however, could not keep pace with the losses. What is more, the Germans launched new submarines faster than Allied warships and aeroplanes could sink them. Unless a solution were found, Britain would grow steadily weaker. It would not be possible to use her as a base for a full-scale offensive against the Reich. Losses were cut by increasing the aircraft carrier escort. Then the new radar apparatus called 'centimetric' began to be used by the escort ships and planes. It permitted the Allies to detect submarines with greater precision from greater distances. It became dangerous for German submarines to surface. In October 1942, the Germans lost thirteen submarines and launched only eleven replacements. In March 1943, Allied losses began to abate. The convoys were the lifeblood of the Allied coalition. The course of the Battle of the Atlantic was about to be reversed, but it was impossible to tell if the change would be permanent or decisive.

Hitler's gravest defeat occurred in Russia where he had engaged larger forces. In July 1942, the Führer defined the capture of Stalingrad as the Wehrmacht's most important objective. The fall of Stalingrad would sever the main north-south supply lines along the Volga. But the name of Stalingrad was itself a challenge to Hitler. Early in August 1942 the German Sixth Army commanded by Paulus reached the fortifications which had been thrown up hurridly outside Stalingrad. On 23 August they arrived at the Volga. Their arrack began on 13 September. A fierce battle ensued. It was fought in streets and houses and especially in the factories, which the Russians used as fortresses. Both sides fought for one building after another, on landings, in rooms, in lift shafts. They fought with hand-grenades and even with bayonets. The Germans had fulfilled their intentions but fought on to capture the entire city as a matter of prestige. Hitler's order assumed that the Russians could not take the offensive before winter. The Soviet command, however, had amassed greater forces than the Germans, particularly in armoured cars. The Russians planned to encircle the German troops inside Stalingrad. They launched their counter-attack on 19 November along a shortened front of 130 miles. The Rumanian divisions were scattered and twenty-two German divisions were surrounded. Instead of ordering a retreat, Hitler ordered his army to break out of the Soviet circle. Von Manstein attempted this on 19 December; his spearhead advanced to within twenty-eight miles of Paulus's army, but Paulus proved too weak to help. The Russians meanwhile defeated the Italian army which had fallen back by 130 miles. The Germans' alternative was to supply their encircled troops by air. They hoped to hold out until spring, but they were decimated by the cold and by illness while the Soviet pincer gradually tightened. Paulus surrendered on 2 February 1943. His army had lost 200,000 men. Another 90,000 including 24 generals were captured.

The German troops which had reached the forts in the Caucasus were also in danger of being cut off. They hurriedly withdrew to Rostov. The Russians recaptured Rostov in February 1943. The myths of the Germans' invincibility and the Fuhrer's infallibility had been discredited. Soviet prestige swelled everywhere in the world, particularly in occupied Europe. In every theatre of the war at the end of 1942 it was no longer clear which side was the stronger or which side would win.

The Anglo-American Collaboration

In organizing their combined effort, the British and the Americans achieved an unprecedented degree of cooperation. The war effort in Britain was officially presided over by a reduced war cabinet, whereas Churchill assumed the major responsibility with the common consent of his colleagues who recognized his inexhaustable energy and his spirit of invention. The chiefs of staff formulated plans based on the Prime Minister's recommendations; then the Prime Minister took the final decision. Constitutionally the same system was followed in America, except that President Roosevelt had to pay greater attention to public opinion. Although Roosevelt and Churchill were very different in character they shared a common attitude towards the importance of their respective roles and duties. They cemented a close friendship which was never shaken by differences of opinion. They communicated regularly with each other by cables between Washington and London. By this means decisions could be taken jointly. The combined chiefs of staff were set up in Washington to draft plans and execute decisions. Their common language did much to facilitate work and to enhance mutual understanding. Cooperation lasted until the end of the war. The British and the Americans did not always agree on strategy or on the future of the world. There were certainly squabbles, but they always managed to reach an agreement.

The two heads of state spelled out their collective war aims in a formal document which was drawn up before the United States entered the war. It was called the Atlantic Charter. All the governments which fought against Germany approved its terms. The Charter affirmed the rights of individuals and the need for cooperation during and after the war. At a meeting at Casablanca in January 1943 Roosevelt and Churchill reached another very important decision concerning their enemies. Although they declared that they were not fighting against the people of Italy, Germany and Japan, but against their governments and their corrupt leaders, they decided, on Roosevelt's suggestion, that no peace would be negotiated unless the enemy acknowledged and conceded defeat in an 'unconditional surrender'. This formula closed the door to possible compromises, but it showed the enemy the energy and fierce resolution with which the Allies were fighting and it gave encouragement to people in occupied countries.

The Russian Front

The political structure of the Soviet Union did not change during the war. The communist party retained power and continued to control the principal posts in government. A special committee, called the State Defence Committee, was created, similar to the Committee of Public Safety. It was without administrative departments and took direct decisions on any matter it chose. It sent out delegates who were empowered to execute the committee's decisions. Stavka, the military headquarters, were responsible for military operations. But Stalin's presence was felt everywhere. He was head of the party, head of the government, and as commander of the army he assumed the title of marshal. With the possible exception of the first days of the German invasion, Stalin responded to events with a bold front and stern realism. He disregarded all but the needs of the government and the country.

In each of the Great Allies, a single man, ironically a civilian, became the figurehead of the war effort. The three men needed to meet face to face, especially as they were suspicious of each other. Soviet Russia was practically alone in bearing the full brunt of the Wehrmacht. Stalin complained bitterly and repeatedly insisted that a second front be opened. He under-estimated obstacles which stood in the way of a second front, but the Americans agreed to land in North Africa in partial satisfaction of his demands. Another difficulty was the delivery of war materials granted Soviet Russia under the Lend-Lease programme. The shortest route lay across the glacial arctic ocean to Murmansk, but it was the most dangerous route. Heavy losses sometimes forced the British to suspend shipments. In order to open a new route, the Allies jointly occupied Iran, but this proved circuitous, railway and road transport were inadequate, and the delays were excessive. Churchill's only concessions to Stalin consisted of promises and an offer of an alliance for twenty years. Stalin was dissatisfied. While the Germans were within range of Moscow, however, he aggravated mutual suspicion by telling Anthony Eden of his intention to keep whatever territories he had gained under the Russo-German Pact. Poland would be the loser. This was only a matter of words for the present. The Americans and the British had more to fear from the defeat of the Red Army or from a new pact between Russia and Germany. Churchill and Roosevelt did not wish to disrupt their 'strange alliance' with Soviet Russia, as it was dubbed by an American diplomat.

The Teheran Conference

The Three Great Powers held their first meeting at Teheran in October 1943, after Italy had surrendered.[15] None of them, especially Stalin, was very outspoken about military plans. They each refused to divulge a great deal or to attempt to coordinate operations. They merely settled the dates on which each would launch an offensive against Germany. The British and Americans agreed to attack across the English Channel. They had not been fully decided before arriving at the conference where they yielded before Stalin's obduracy. Their most important discussions had to do with policy after the war. Only Stalin had formulated precise plans for Germany and Poland.

The Three Great Powers concurred that Germany should be punished for provoking the war and for using criminal methods to fight it. Germany would be occupied, her territory drastically reduced, her economy and especially heavy industry restricted, and she would be partitioned. Only the new countries remained to be discussed and their borders hammered out. Although Stalin agreed to these more general plans, he affirmed that it was Nazism and not Germany which had to be destroyed. He opposed Churchill's suggestion to resuscitate the Austro-Hungarian Empire in the form of a Danubian Confederation. He had other plans for these areas, but he kept them to himself.

Poland presented the thorniest problem. The British had gone to war in the first place in defence of Polish borders. Roosevelt could not disregard a significant Polish minority in the United States. The legitimate Polish government in London had tried to reach an understanding with Stalin and a Polish army was mustered from Polish prisoners taken by the Red Army, but negotiations broke down after the Katyn massacre was discovered. Without consulting the Polish government Roosevelt and Churchill accepted in principle that Poland's eastern frontier would follow the Curzon Line of 1918. Soviet Russia would retain the territory annexed in September 1939, but Poland would be granted ample compensation at Germany's expense in the form of East Prussia, Pomerania and Silesia. This arrangement provided a pretext for Stalin to claim Koenigsberg, which had never previously been Russian.

The British War Effort

By Autumn 1943, mobilization of resources had progressed to a reassuring level and the Allies were in a position to discuss plans for after the war.

The British war effort was typical in a number of ways. 'Industrial conscription' was authorized by law. The whole of the British public uncomplainingly accepted hard work in factories, rationing, increased taxes and reduced living standards. These burdens were offset by a promise of sweeping social reform under the Beveridge plan for universal social security. At best, however, British capacities were limited. The mobilization of labour syphoned manpower from the fighting force while the limited output of maximum production restricted fighting strength still further. Only 7400 tanks and 26,000 aeroplanes were produced in 1943; and slightly fewer in 1944. The Commonwealth made a significant contribution, but it turned out to be smaller than had been hoped. South Africa confined her operations to Africa, while Austrialia had to keep back forces for her own defence. The failure of negotiations with the Indian nationalist leaders put a brake on India's contributions. On the other hand, Canada made a substantial contribution, despite the French Canadians reluctance: a million men were enlisted.

The Arsenal of Democracy

The Canadian economy was gradually merged with that of the United States, while the American economy shadowed forth unlimited potential. According to Roosevelt's plan, America became the 'arsenal of democracy'. But in 1939 she was still feeling the effects of the Great Depression of the 1930's. There were seven million unemployed and her preparation for war was feeble. Her army had only 190,000 men, with 330 light tanks, almost no air force. Only her navy was powerful. Munitions constituted two per cent of total production.

On the whole public opinion in America actively opposed participation in the war and rearmament. A number of politicians and some great industrialists such as Ford were in the forefront of America First, the American non-alliance movement. After Pearl Harbour, a large, modern, diversified war industry had to be created, and millions of men had to be armed, trained and dispatched thousands of miles, with them supplies, amounting to a ton per head. Arms had to be furnished to Allies in difficulties, who amounted to nearly all the enemies of the Axis. New ships had to be built to transport these arms. A few of Roosevelt's advisors urged him to centralize the war effort. Without centralized controls, they argued, America's very ambitious programme could not be carried out and many pitfalls could not be avoided. Although the President's role was vital, he was reluctant to clash with American temperament and habits. He initiated the Victory Programme, which appealed to Americans' sense of enterprise by setting astronomic goals for war production. In 1942, for example, it included 60,000 aeroplanes and 40,000 tanks; in 1943, 125,000 planes and 75,000 tanks. These totalled more than all the rest of the world possessed together.

An administrative system – the 'services' – was improvised to deal with the distribution of raw materials and of labour, to regulate and direct production, to purchase goods, to oversee profit margins and to regulate prices and incomes. Controls were unlimited, but they were discreetly applied. Manufacture of motor cars and refrigerators, for example, was merely restricted. Ports were taken over by a military administration. Frauds were investigated and punished. Ceilings were placed on prices. Certain markets were examined regularly. These regulations, which were fixed temporarily and continuously revised, vanished at the end of the war. The growth of State expenditure from $13,000 million in 1939 to $71,000 million in 1944 carried a threat of inflation, which was modulated by a programme of low-interest borrowing. Although some goods were rationed, the Americans generally succeeded in producing sufficient 'guns and butter' simultaneously. Most private enterprises benefited lavishly but salaries did not increase in the same degree. Despite the co-operation of the trade union leaders, some strikes could not be avoided. Taken as a whole, however, the economy boomed. In 1942 only 746 merchant ships, or 'liberty ships' as they were called, were built, but production swelled to 2242 in the next year. Sixteen per cent of total production was sent to the Allies under the Lend-lease programme, including shipments of 4,400 tanks and 6,800 planes in 1942.

The Mobilization in Soviet Russia

The Soviet economy was reorganized in an entirely different way. The Germans invaded the regions where most of the metal industry was concentrated, causing a drop in total production of forty-eight per cent in the first six months of the war, and further declined in 1942. Cast iron production fell from 18 million tons to 5 million tons. On the other hand, under a policy of continuous growth in the years before the war, many factories had been constructed in the Urals and beyond. Soviet Russia could draw upon almost unlimited reserves of manpower, though it was largely untrained. Because of her size, large areas were safe from enemy attack. Her political and economic system allowed stern measures to be quickly applied. Before the invasion, the government had examined the problem of evacuating factories and residents eastwards away from areas threatened by invasion. Fully fitted stand-ins had already been prepared for some industries. Still the undertaking was gigantic. Between July and November 1941, some 1520 units of production including 1300 large establishments, were disassembled, transported and reassembled. Ten million workers had to be resettled. By the end of 1941 the factories which had been transferred from Leningrad to the Urals began sending heavy tanks to the front. War industries took precedence over everything else. By the end of 1942, Soviet Russia was turning out more guns than Germany.

Such an effort entailed immense toil and hardship. Working hours were lengthened, holidays were entirely suspended. The hurried evacuation of populations gave rise to painful living conditions and shortages of housing, hospitals, heating and schools. Food was also scarce. The training of urgently needed skilled labour presented one of the most difficult tasks. Prio-

American War Economy and Production

	1939	1941	1942	1943	1944	1945
Gross national product (million $)	91.4	126.4	161.6	194.3	213.7	215.2
Industrial output (1935–39 = 100)	109	162	199	239	235	203
Retail prices (1935–39 = 100)	99.4	105.2	116.5	123.6	125.5	128.4
Wholesale prices (1926 = 100)	77.1	87.3	98.8	103.1	104	105.8
Workers (in millions)	45.7	50.3	53.7	54.5	54	52.8
Working hours per week	37.7	40.6	43.9	44.9	45.2	43.4
Share prices based on 416 shares (1935–39 = 100)	94.2	80	69.4	91.9	99.8	121.5
National income (billion $)	6.7	15.7	23.2	39.6	41.6	43
National expenditure (billion $)	9	20.5	56.1	86	95.6	84.4
National debt (billion $)	42	58	108.2	165.9	230.6	278
Government purchase of goods and services (billion $)	13.1	24.7	59.7	88.6	96.5	82.8
National defence only	5.2	13.8	49.6	80.4	88.6	76
Personal income (billion $)	72.6	95.3	122.7	150.3	165.9	171.9
Mobilized forces at 1 January[a] (thousands)	0.4	1.5	5	6.8	7.2	7.4
Production of ships[b] (million tons)	1.5	2.5	7	16	16.3	
Production of tanks	346[b]	4,052	24,997	29,497	17,565	20,000[c]
Production of planes	2,141	19,433	47,836	85,898	96,318	46,000[d]

[a] Army and air force only, and counting mobilized men only; with the navy and other services 12 million were mobilized.
[b] Figures given are for 1940.
[c] Approximate.
[d] Nine months only.

rities had to be established and workers were given obligatory assignments. A large number of *kolkhozin* were given jobs in the mines. A programme of training skilled workers was undertaken in schools. Arms production was increased and the quality of equipment improved. New tanks and aeroplanes – T34's and Stormoviks – replaced older models.

In Soviet Russia, the entire population was drawn into the

Soviet War Production

	1940	1941 (1st 6 mo.)	1942	1943	1944	1945 (10 mo.)
Iron (molten million tons)	14.9	9.1	5	5.5	7.2	8.8
Part produced in eastern Russia	28%					
Steel (million tons)	18.3	11.4	4.8	8.4	10.8	12.2
Part produced in eastern Russia	37%					
Rolled iron million tons)	13.1	8.2	5.4	5.6	7.8	8.4
Military planes (modern)	a few dozen	3,950	25,437	34,900	40,301	26,478
Tanks (and machine-gun mounted cars)	2,794	4,742	24,668	24,000	29,000	22,590
Pieces of artillery	29,561	130,000	122,000	77,000		
Manpower (in millions)	30	26.2	18,4	27.5		

a Figure for second half of 1941.

war effort. A vigorous propaganda programme recalled great examples of the past, especially 1812, emphasizing the invasion of national territory over defence of the regime. The three million members of the Communist Party trained the population, galvanized their energies, rallied support in the occupied areas. Soldiers, victims of German aggression, producers behind the lines, each bore a share of the national burden. The residents of Leningrad themselves built the fortifications around their city. In Stalingrad munitions workers drove the tanks which they themselves had produced into battle.

The Allied Strategy in Europe and Asia

Once the Allies had organized their full resources in the war effort, their superiority in arms gave them the chance to win. Their task was to put their arms to good use. Since the theatres of the war were separate, a lack of coordination among them was not a serious problem. Each assessed its position and planned its strategy as it judged best. Only the Americans and the British were obliged to coordinate operations, at least in Western Europe and in Africa.

Soviet Russia's first objective was to liberate her occupied territories. When the Red Army regained the Soviet frontiers, the Russians would have the chance to consider alternatives and to introduce political considerations into their decisions. Until then strategy was straightforward; they applied a steam-roller principle. Stavka distributed its superior fighting force and its increasingly superior arms according to the forces of the enemy, driving the battering ram first against weak points held by troops from Germany's satellites. Three thousand men, nine tanks and sixty guns were concentrated into every kilometer of a relatively narrow front. As they burst through the enemy line a fresh assault was launched elsewhere. This method of attack required rapid mobility of large forces and adroit control of logistics. It was skilfully employed by a battery of newly appointed marshals.

The Americans resolved to give priority to the conquest of Germany, much to the encouragement of the British. The final assault on Japan would begin after Germany had fallen. They assigned considerably smaller forces to the Pacific theatre than to Europe and these required special training for jungle warfare. The decisive battles, however, occurred at sea. The Americans assumed command of Pacific operations and divided them in two. The southern zone, which comprised many widely scattered islands, was apportioned to the Army. General MacArthur, who was in command, would advance from island to island in an 'island hopping' campaign as far as the Philippines, where he had promised to return. The central area, in which ocean predominated, was assigned to the navy. Naval squadrons were furnished with large numbers of aircraft carriers under orders to wipe out the Japanese fleet and clear the way for a final assault on the Japanese archipelago. In 1943 it was impossible to tell when or where this would occur. A secondary front was formed in China, which was accessible only to American aviation. British cooperation was not needed outside Burma.

But cooperation was indispensable in Europe and Africa. The two allies shared out operations giving the British command of the Mediterranean and the Americans command of operations in western Europe. The Atlantic was left undivided. The two allies held long discussions on how to launch their combined offensive. The British wanted to return to limited attacks on the German periphery in Norway, the Balkans and Italy. The Americans, on the other hand, who were aware of their increasing power, preferred to attack the Germans directly from across the English Channel using Britain as a springboard. They agreed to campaign in North Africa and Italy, however, while the assault force was being assembled.

1　German tanks parade before Brandenberg Gate.

2 The Japanese conquest in China. A tank unit advancing in Hunan.

3 October 1939. The Germans bomb Warsaw.

4 The German occupation of Norway. The *Prince Eugen* advancing down a fjord.

5 Germans occupy the debris-laden beach at Dunkirk after British and French have withdrawn.

6 The indiscriminate bombing of London. Firemen at work at Eastcheap.

7 The aftermath of the German bombardment of London. Air-raid damage looking down from St. Paul's, January 1941.

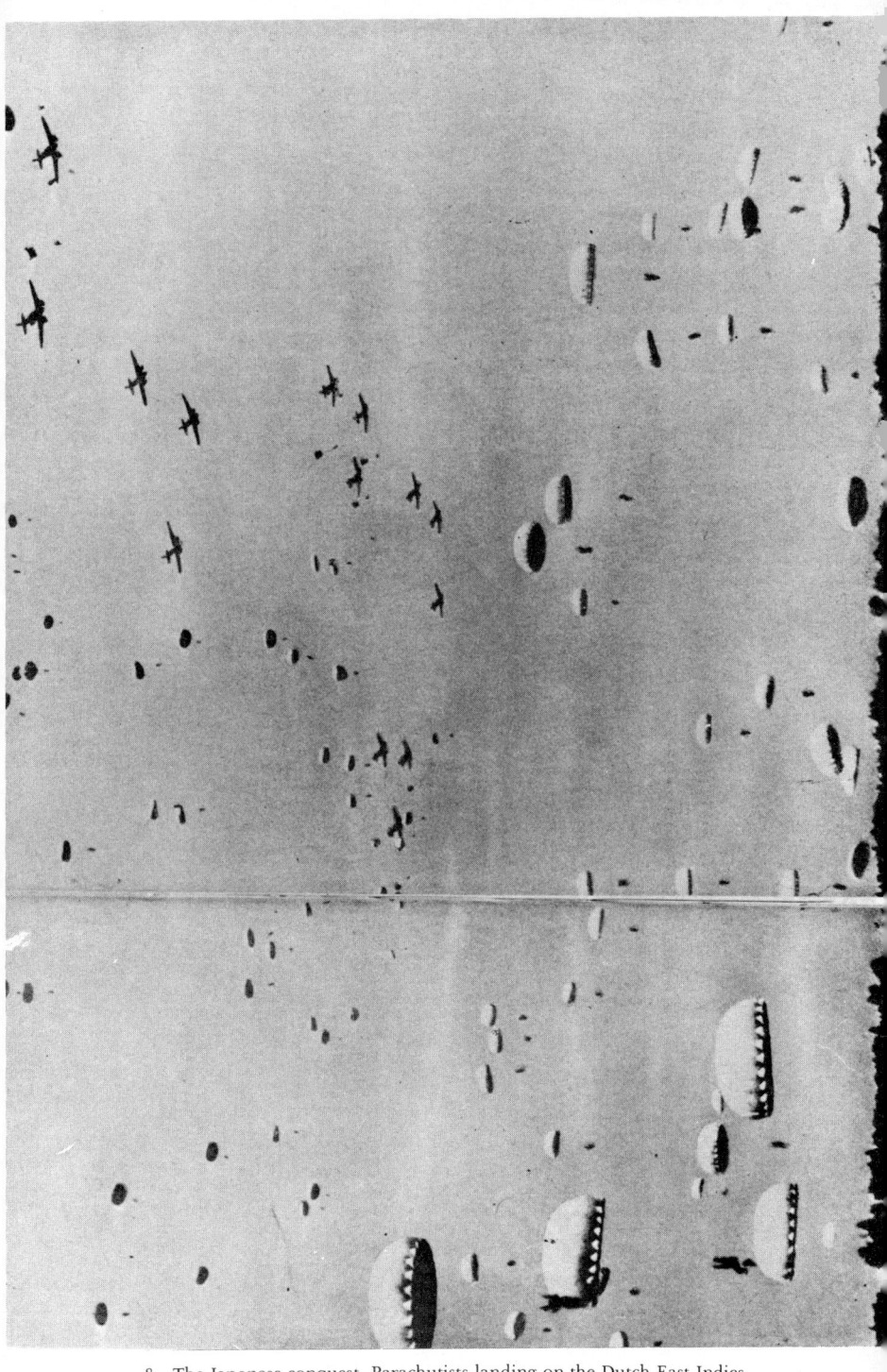
8 The Japanese conquest. Parachutists landing on the Dutch East Indies.

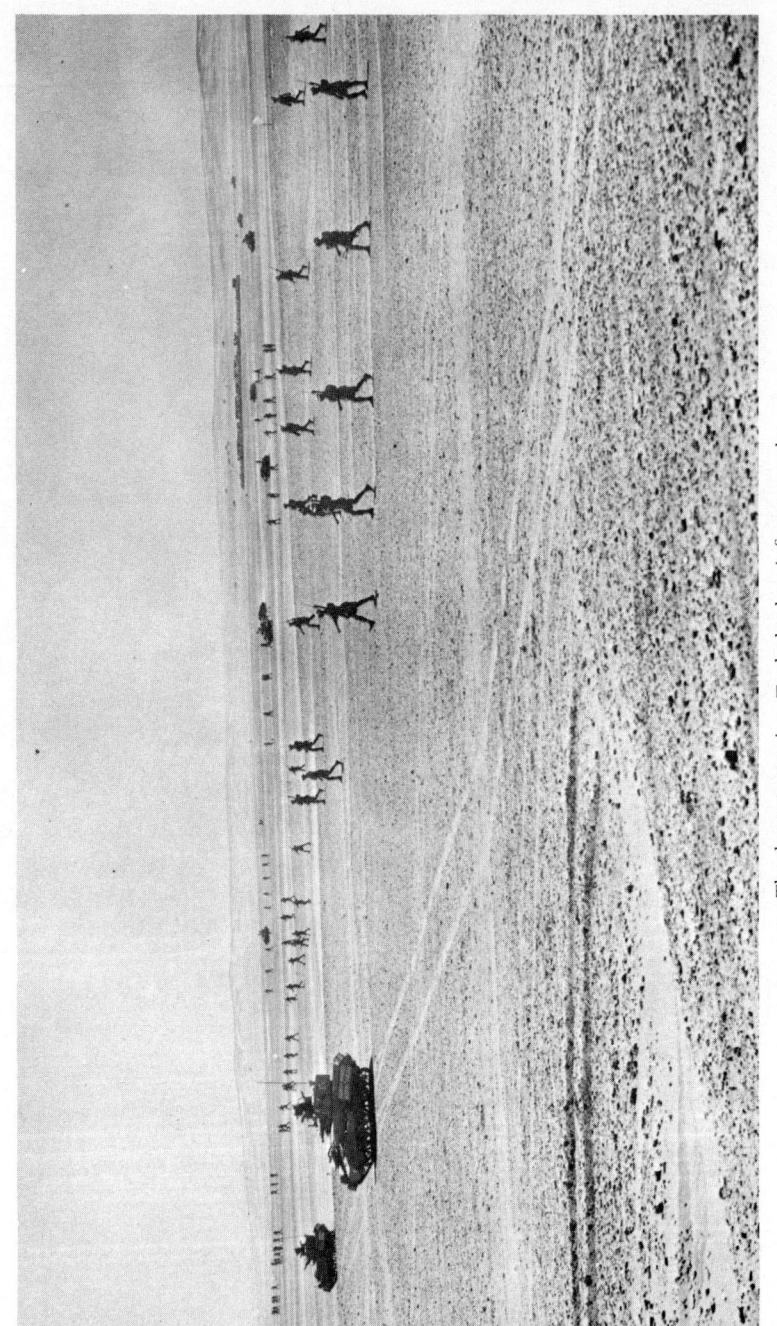

9 The desert campaign. Tanks lead an infantry attack.

10 The wireless becomes a propaganda tool. A German long-range photo of transmitters on the English coast near Dover.

11 Governments used propaganda to boost morale and strengthen resolve.

12 Propaganda was also used to discredit the enemy and weaken morale. A leaflet dropped on England early in the war.

13 The invasion of Soviet Russia. German photograph of a bombing raid on a Black Sea port.

14 The Resistance. A photograph of Russian guerillas plotting strategy, showing the typical features of the Resistance, limited equipment, no uniforms, high risk.

15 The Soviet counter-offensive. Anti-aircraft guns in the Russian winter.

16 Merchant shipping was vital to the Allied strategy. A North Sea convoy carrying supplies to Soviet Russia.

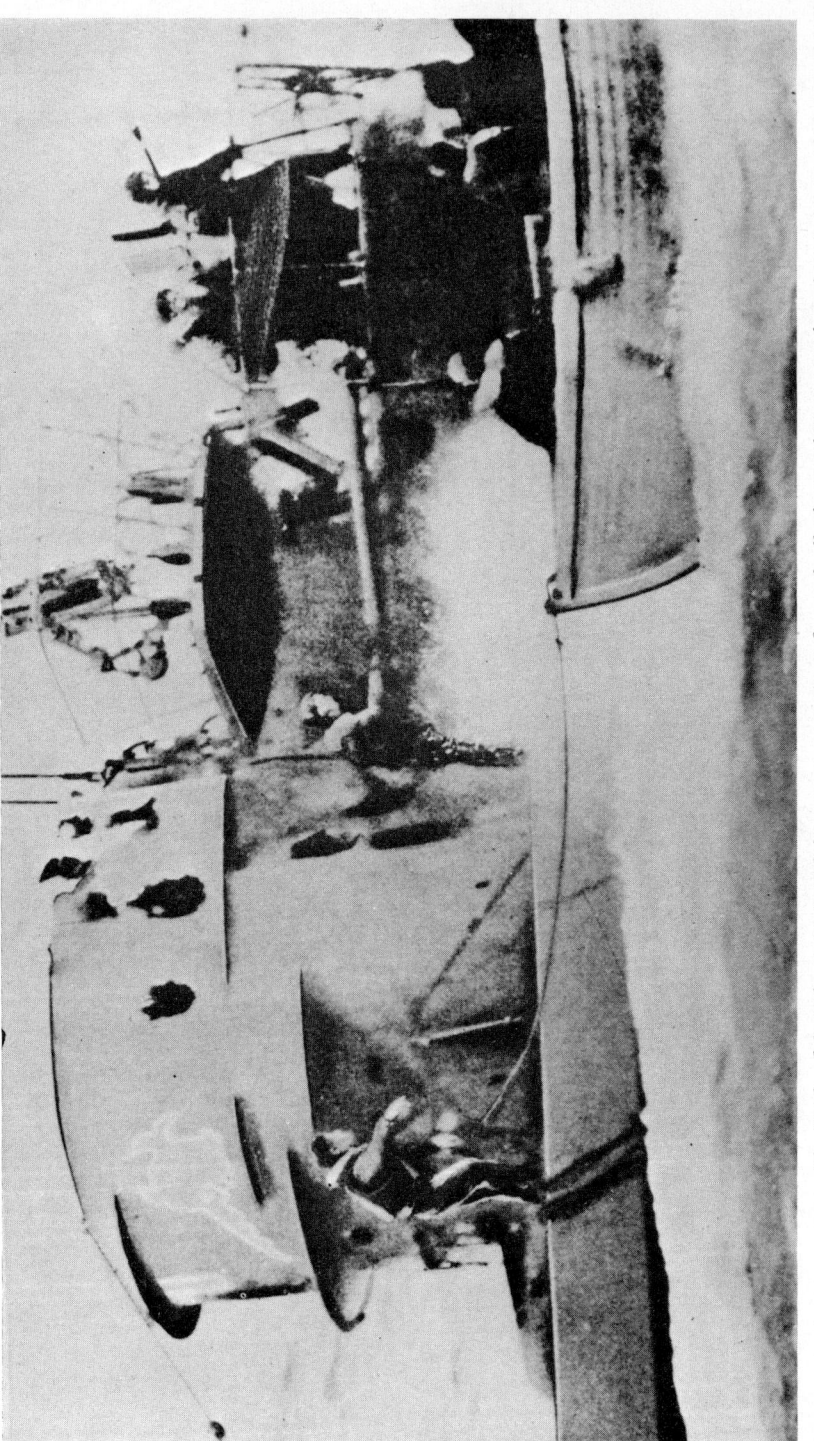

17 The Battle of the Atlantic. A British boat rescues survivors from a badly damaged German submarine.

18 Prisoners of war numbered in the millions. British prisoners marched off by Germans after the unsuccessful raid on Dieppe, August 1942.

19 A typical image of a P.O.W. camp, Stalag Luft 3 in Silesia.

20 The aftermath of the Warsaw uprising in November 1944. Most of Warsaw was destroyed.

21 One of the pre-fabricated harbours used in the Normandy landing to facilitate the unloading of over a million men, and supplies and ammunition.

22 Troops wade ashore from an amphibious craft at Normandy, June 1944.

23 U.S. bombers drop bombs in formation.

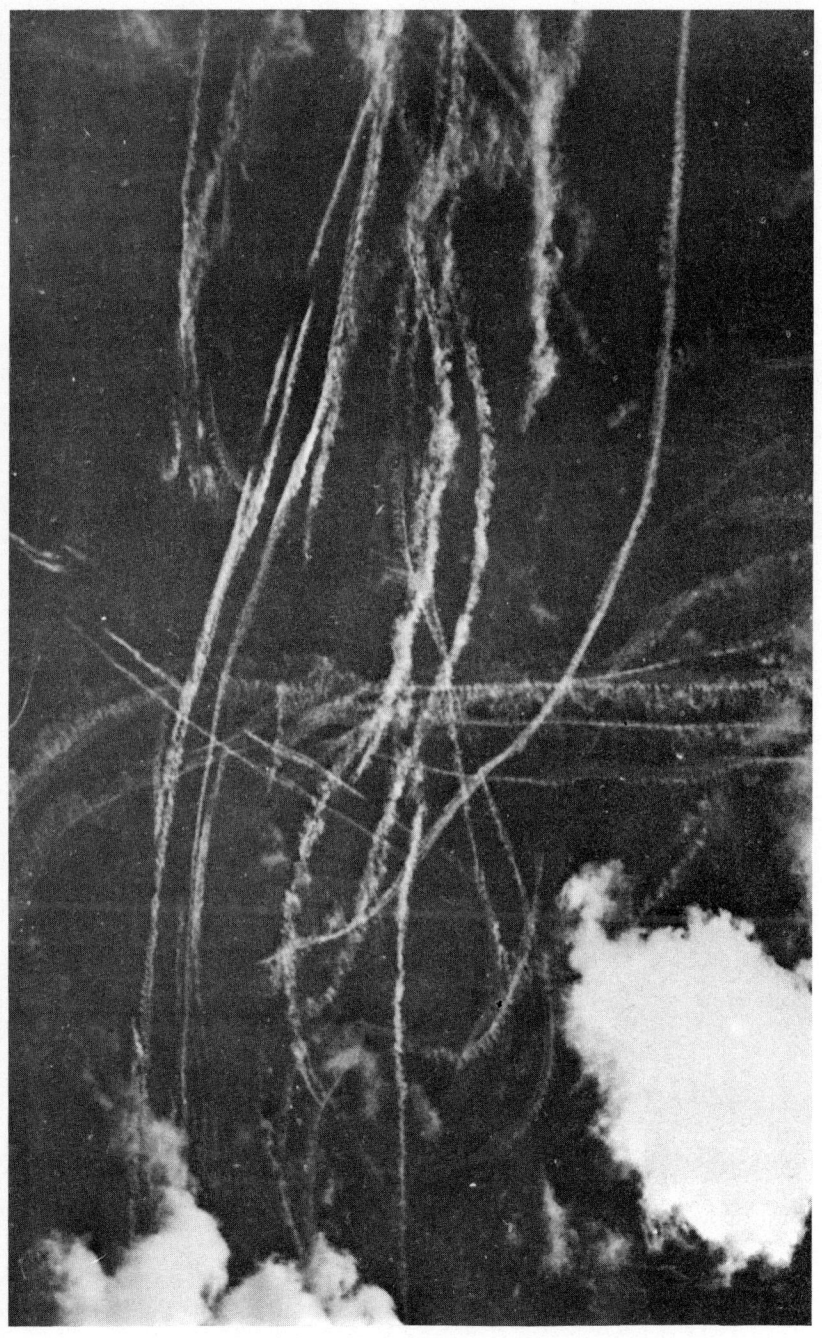
24 Vapour trails left by fighters in aerial combat as seen from the ground.

25 Press photo of Allied and Soviet troops joining up at Torgau, 25 April 1945, for the final assault on Berlin.

26 The war in the Pacific. Australian troops reconquer New Guinea from the Japanese.

27 The American Pacific Fleet riding at anchor.

28 The American landing at Iwo Jima, a vital step in the defeat of Japan.

29 The recapture of the Philippines. Americans engage Japanese ships off the Philippine coast.

30 The atom bomb. Photograph taken over Nagasaki just after the second atom bomb had been detonated over Japan.

31 The aftermath of the atom bomb. Photograph taken a half-mile from the centre of explosion looking away from the centre across the desolate remains of the city of Hiroshima.

IV The Allied Victory

The Tunisian Campaign

The Americans overcautiously rejected a plan to land in Tunisia. The Germans seized the occasion, and the Allies were forced to undertake a Tunisian campaign which they might otherwise have avoided, so prolonging the African campaign. The Germans took advantage of the state of confusion into which the French had fallen at Tunis and at Bizerta, and formed a bridgehead. Their purpose was to save Rommel's Afrika Korps, which was retreating continuously westward before the British Eighth Army under Montgomery. The Allies decided not to capture Tunis and concentrated their attacks on the Italian and German troops. The Americans occupied the northern front, the French the middle and the British the southern front. Only a fraction of the Italo-German force embarked and escaped, while 250,000 Italians were captured at Cap Bon. Montgomery was supported by a token force of Free French troops from Chad under the command of Leclerc. The French army of the armistice thus satisfied its wish to regain a place in the Allied force, although it lacked equipment and could not avoid some sense of divided loyalties. It was gradually fitted out with American arms and retained for modern warfare, and was later given the chance to redeem the defeat of 1940, first in Italy and then in Provence.

But France was not completely committed to the Allies and disunity among the French did not help. After the short mysterious command of Admiral Darlan, there was a long dispute as to

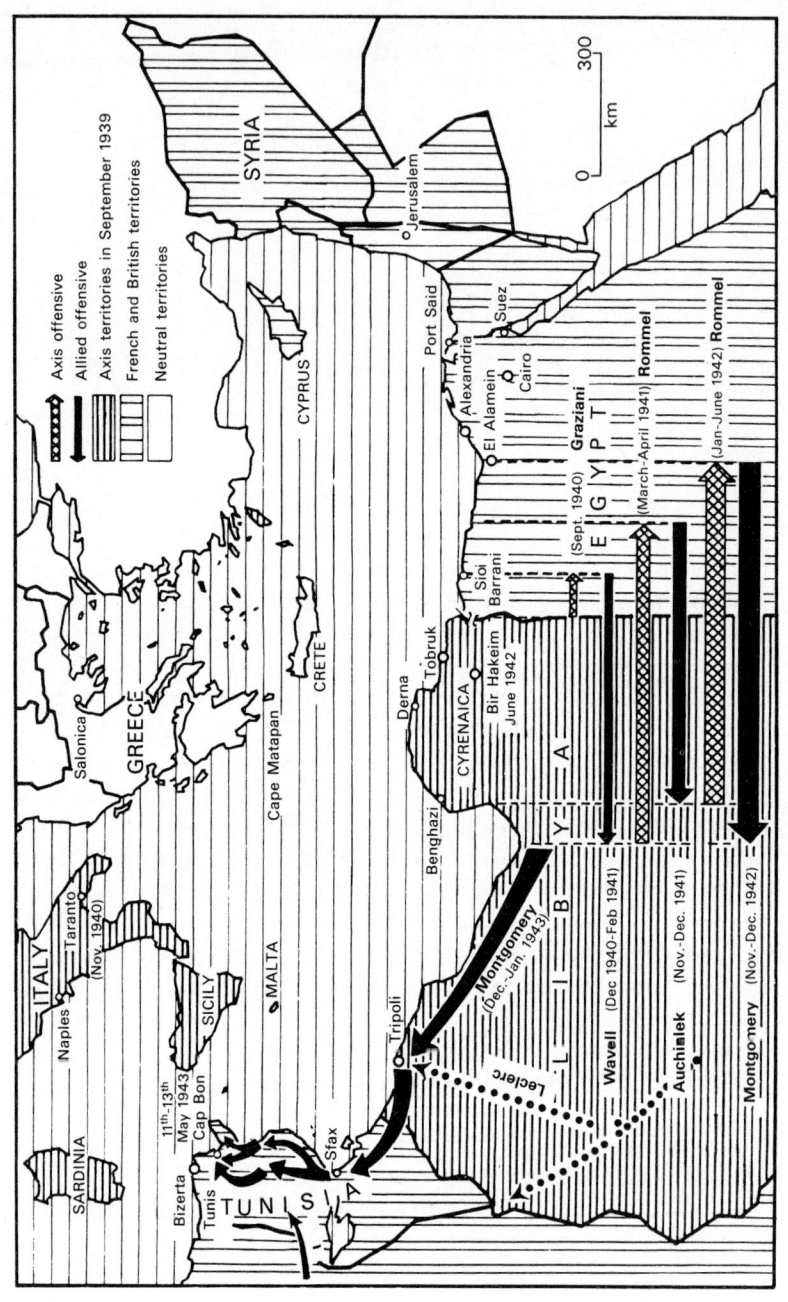

The war in Africa and in the Mediterranean.

whether he should be succeeded by General Giraud, who was backed by the Americans, or by General de Gaulle, who was favoured by the Resistance. The two candidates agreed to combine forces in a single army and to establish a joint command, the French Committee of National Liberation, from which General Giraud was gradually edged out. At Algiers, which was made the capital of the Free French, the Committee organized an immense effort to mobilize all the resources of the French Empire and to modify the colonies' status, to help the resistance inside France, to restore a republican constitution and repeal the laws of the Vichy government, to prepare to assume power in France and to execute sweeping reforms which would resuscitate France after the war. The Americans largely disapproved of this effort and they would recognize none but the *de facto* government in France.

The Italian Campaign

In January 1943 at Casablanca, Roosevelt and Churchill decided to force Italy out of the war. A landing in Sicily in July 1943 cleared the east-west route across the Mediterranean. The island was captured within a month, but the German troops escaped. It was obvious that Italy had exhausted her resources. She had lost her empire. Her navy had been immobilized in its bases and was vulnerable to air attack. She could not withstand invasion. Industrial production had fallen by thirty-five per cent, while currency in circulation had trebled. Fascism had become increasingly unpopular as the Duce's physical and intellectual powers declined. Mussolini was not overthrown by his enemies, however, but by his supporters. On 24 July the Fascist Grand Council voted to 'restore the constitution'. In effect it dismissed Mussolini and restored absolute powers to the king. Victor Emanuel, with a few army chiefs, had resolved that Italy should stop fighting and reverse her alliances.

He deposed Mussolini and then overcautiously ordered his arrest and imprisonment.

Marshal Badoglio was appointed head of the government. While assuring the Germans that he would remain faithful to the Axis, he opened secret negotiations with the Allies which ended with Italy's unconditional surrender on 3 September 1943, made public on 8 September.

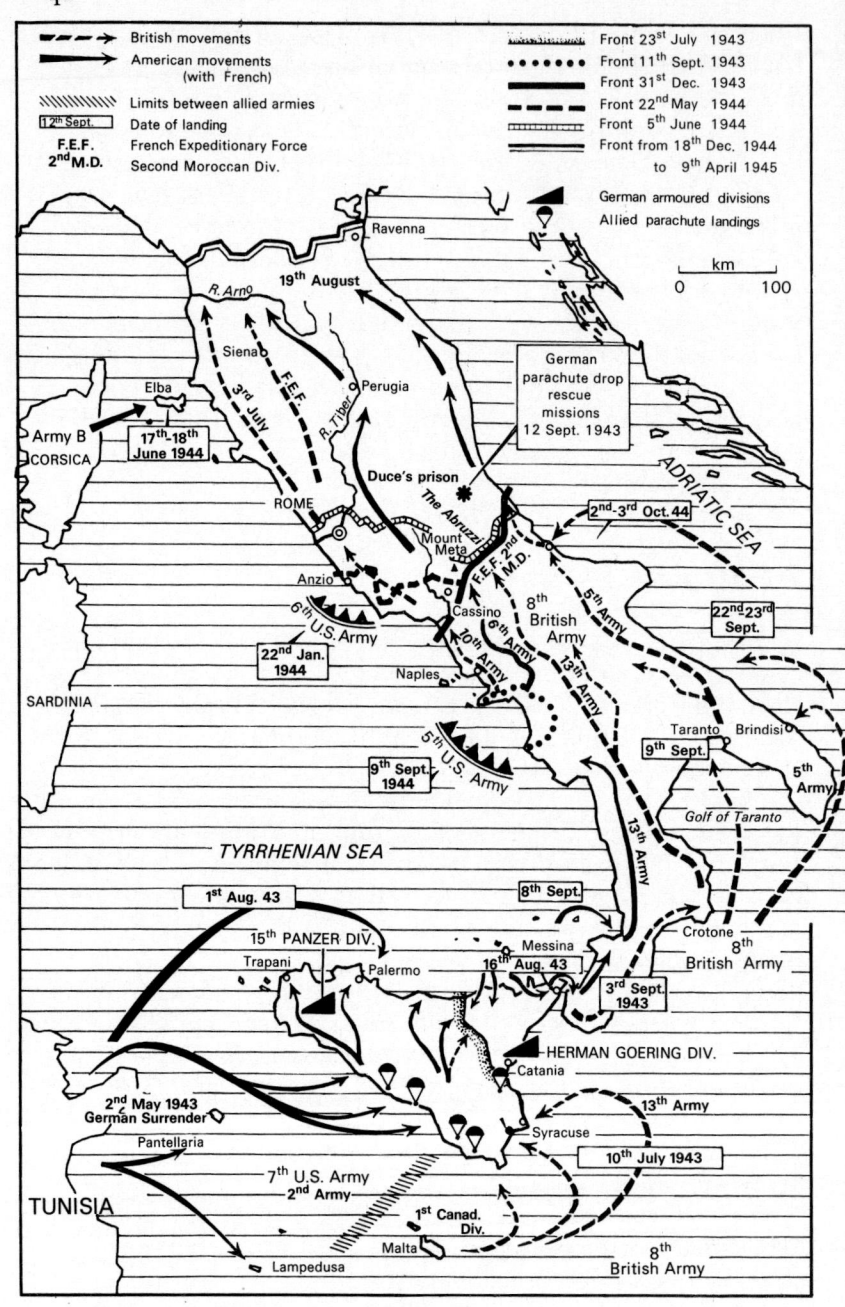

The Italian Campaign.

The surrender caused great confusion in Italy. The Allied troops under General Eisenhower's command did not penetrate north of Naples, and Germans who had been prepared for Italy to defect, immediately occupied northern and central Italy, including Rome.

Without great difficulty they disarmed the Italian troops in Italy and in the other occupied territories. But the Italian fleet escaped and surrendered to the Allies. The King and Badoglio fled to Brindisi where they attempted to ingratiate themselves with the Allies. As they lacked power, however, the Allies regarded them as enemies and the occupied territories were placed under martial law.

Two new factors changed the situation. First Mussolini was released by SS parachutists. With his remaining supporters, he formed a Fascist republic at Salo in the north. He executed his son-in-law Ciano for having deserted him on 24 July.

Second, anti-fascism surfaced throughout Italy. Exiles returning to Italy formed a new clandestine resistance movement, which fought both the Germans and the fascists. But they also fought the King and Badoglio, whom the Allies had accepted into their camp so as to keep a rein on them.

Civil war ensued. In the liberated zone Badoglio quelled it by rallying the communists and admitting the leaders of the resistance into the Bonomi government; but in the sectors occupied by the Germans a full-scale war raged.

A battle for position was fought from the south, northwards along the peninsula. The terrain was compartmentalized by mountains. It favoured defensive operations and cancelled out the Allied superiority in tanks and planes. The region around Monte Cassino witnessed particularly bitter fighting. The Allies, including a French expeditionary force under Juin, landed at Anzio in January 1944. They did not reach Rome until 4 June, or Ravenna until December. The Italian surrender opened the way for Corsica to be liberated. In September 1943, French assault batallions were landed. They took the island in a combined operation with resistance fighters.

The Bombing of Germany

Mussolini's fall and the surrender of Italy had a profound effect on morale. Neither event altered Germany's military power, except by delivering her of a weak and cumbersome ally. Although a few fighting divisions had been diverted from the Russian front, Russia continued to bear the brunt of the German offensive. Stalin regarded the Italian front as a mere sham and repeated his demands for a real second front.

Southern Italian airfields were within bombing range of German territory. The Allies expected bombing to accomplish miracles by reducing war production and so depriving the army of equipment, weakening morale and hastening the end of the war. The bombers had progressively increased their range and their precision, while the weight and the number of bombs dropped had been growing steadily from 48,000 tons in 1942, to 207,000 tons in 1943 to 915,000 tons in 1944. Targets were shared between the British and Americans. The British concentrated on indescriminate area bombing covering all the Reich's large cities, while the Americans attacked more specific military and economic targets. These methods seemed to work. They reduced the Reich to rubble. But much to the Allies' surprise, German arms production grew steadily up to the end of 1944. Speer, the great overseer of German munitions industries, dispersed and camouflaged factories and workshops. The bombing did paralyse thousands of anti-aircraft guns in Germany and prevented hundreds of thousands of gunners from reaching the Russian front. It brought transport to a standstill and halted the flow of raw material and arms. It spread terror and defeatism among the civil populations and among soldiers at the front, who knew that their families at home were under attack. But on its own bombing could not win the war.

The gradual decline of German fighting strength had complex causes. Because the Germans had planned on a short war, their arms industry was not as modern and could not produce as large quantities as the Allies'. Hitler's decisions also weakened them. He postponed development of jet fighter planes, which might have reversed the air battles to Germany's advantage. He concentrated on bombers so as to retaliate against Britain for the bombs dropped on Germany. Rivalry between the forces – Goering's management of the Luftwaffe – made it difficult to co-ordinate production. The Nazi doctrine of the 'woman at the hearth' prohibited employment of German women. Above all, after Russia's industry had been mobilized, the combined power of Germany's enemies was invincible, despite Germany's exploitation of European resources. Germany was defeated by numbers. Yet Hitler never gave up hope of victory. Until the very last moment, his troops fought savagely, sometimes fanatically, especially on the eastern front.

The Landings in Normandy and Provence

At the Teheran conference, the Allies agreed to launch a full-scale offensive against Germany from across the English Channel. It was called the Overlord Plan and placed under General Eisenhower's command. Seventy-five thousand ships transported 4 million men, mostly from America, but also from Canada, and 280 million tons of arms and material to Britain, where they joined forces with the British army. Normandy was chosen as the landing point. On 6 June 1944, despite a howling storm, 4,300 transport ships, preceded by 300 minesweepers and escorted by 500 warships discharged five divisions at five separate points. Three other divisions were dropped by parachute. The 'Atlantic Wall' could not withstand the assault. The Germans had been misinformed about where the landing would occur, and no longer had enough submarines to obstruct it. They lost time by concentrating their troops in order to contain the Allied forces, while the Allies won complete mastery of the air. The major German forces were pinned down by the British near Caen. The Americans meanwhile occupied the Cotentin peninsula and thrust southwards, reaching Avranches on 1 August. As reinforcements poured into an artificial harbour at Arromanches the Allied troops north of the Loire veered eastwards towards the Seine. On 15 August a second landing was made in Provence. Churchill tried unsuccessfully to cancel it and divert the force to Italy where a stalemate had been reached. A French army commanded by Delattre de Tassigny took part in the Provence landing and occupied Marseilles and Toulon. The Germans fled northwards from the pincer; and the Allies chased them as far as Lorraine.

The French Forces of the Interior emerged from hiding. They scouted for the landing forces, harassed the German retreat, and liberated cities in the van of the Allied advance. At Paris they rallied a popular uprising which was then successfully carried through by the Second Armoured Division under General Leclerc. A provisional government under General de Gaulle was formed at Paris and assembled the leaders of the Resistance and set up a new administration, prosecuted collaborators and silenced revolutionary outbursts, mostly in the southwest. It carried out a certain number of plans which had been laid by in the resistance movement or in Algiers, most notably the fusion of the 140,000 French Forces of the Interior with the French First Army.

The British and the Americans again failed to see eye to eye about stragety. Montgomery wanted to lead the main bulk of the Allied forces in a concerted thrust across the northern plain into the centre of Germany. Eisenhower preferred to advance the whole front uniformly, leaving the line of the final assault to be determined according to what conditions they encountered. The question was settled by the failure of a huge parachute operation at Arnhem in September 1944. The Allies confined their operation to clearing the mouth of the River Scheldt and freeing the port of Antwerp. Troops were advanced as far as the banks of the Meuse and the Siegfried Line, while Lorraine was liberated. Leclerc took Strasbourg and Delattre reached the Rhine near Mulhouse, but the Germans retained control of the Colmar pocket in central Alsace.

The Victories of the Red Army

On the eastern front, the Red Army formed a broad front and advanced still more rapidly over a wider area. At the end of the winter of 1942–1943, the German divisions in the south had retreated to the Donetz. Hitler decided to smooth out the resulting salient. In July, 65 German divisions, including 14 armoured divisions, launched Operation Citadel in the region of Kursk. It became one of the biggest battles in the war in which nearly 3,000 tanks took part. After a confused struggle the German attack was repelled. The tide had turned. Now was the Red Army's turn to unleash an unremitting series of attacks in the seven 'fronts' or groups of armies. The heaviest offensives were launched during the summer but pressure was maintained throughout the winter. During the summer and autumn of 1943 the Russian front between Smolensk and the Black Sea, reached and forded the Dnieper, and proceded to capture Smolensk, Briansk, Kharkov, Kiev and the whole of the Don Basin, cutting off the Crimea. The front had advanced between 200 and 250 miles.

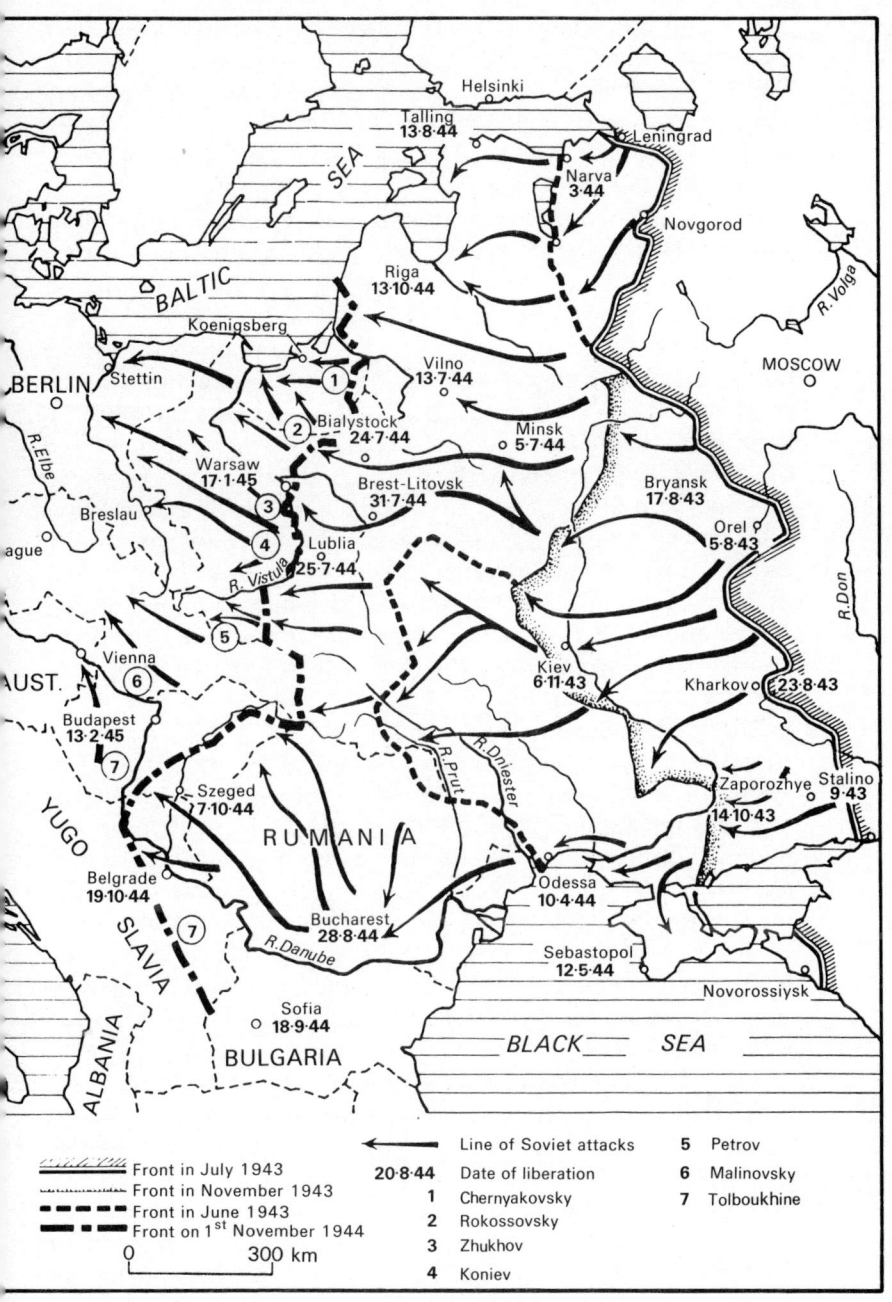

The Counter-offensives of the Red Army.

During the winter 1943–1944 fighting continued in every sector and Leningrad was liberated. In spring Zhukhov and Koniev launched a massive offensive towards the Carpathian Mountains, and they crossed the Dniester and the Prut. On 10 April Odessa fell and the Russians were threatening to enter Rumania. Then the Crimea was liberated. By June the front had stretched to Kovno, Tarnopol and Jassy forming an enormous salient. Hitler uselessly transferred and dismissed his generals. He forbade retreat, which he regarded as insubordination, but he could not prevent the Red Army renewing its offensive along an 800 mile front. It deployed 16,000 aeroplanes and 14,000 tanks, including a new heavy tank called the Joseph Stalin, which outclassed the German tanks. On 2 September, with the southern flank of Finland under fire, Marshal Mannerheim surrendered on Soviet terms. In Bielorussia, the Red Army comprised two and one-half million men. They were supported by 45,000 heavy guns. Soviet superiority was immense. They were able to advance thirteen miles a day. Marshal Rokossovksy took Minsk, Vilno, Bialystock, Lublin, Brest-Litovsk in an uninterrupted advance of 400 miles. On 1 August his army reached the right bank of the Vistula opposite Warsaw, where it had to cope with political obstacles rather than military ones.

The Polish government in London had not recognized Russia's claim to the eastern provinces of Poland. It was unanimously supported by the Polish people. Stalin responded by forming the Lublin Committee, a rival government composed of Polish communists. In July it was installed in the disputed territories and it formally agreed to cede them to Russia. It also reapportioned land among the peasants and raised an army. Without informing the Allies the Polish government in London ordered a general uprising. They wanted to confront the Russians with a Polish government already victoriously in power when they reached Warsaw. Rokossovsky, whether because he lacked the resources or because he had been forbidden, did not cross the Vistula. On 2 October, after two months of heroic struggle, the uprising at Warsaw succumbed. The Germans destroyed the entire city and deported 350,000 inhabitants.

Further south the Slovak rising also failed, but political and military developments in Rumania and Bulgaria were more favourable to Soviet Russia. The leaders of both countries first tried unsuccessfully to get through to the British and Americans, then switched sides. King Michael dismissed General Antonescu on 23 August. Soviet Russia granted a chastened armistice to the Rumanian Army, which immediately busied itself with the task of taking Transylvania back from Hungary. In Bulgaria, after a communist putsch at Sofia, the Red Army entered the capital on 18 September and the Bulgarian Army shifted its allegiance against Germany. Stalin's policies began to add up. He used the German satellites against Germany while bringing them under Soviet influence. This plan failed in Hungary, where Admiral Horthy's vacillations gave the Germans the chance to step in and deposed him in October 1944.

The Defeat and Surrender of Germany

By the end of the winter of 1944, Hitler's Europe had dwindled to very little. On the Eastern front, East Prussia had fallen and the Wehrmacht was left with a few bits of Poland, Hungary, and Italy and nearly all of Czechoslovakia. In the west, the outlook was as grave. Except for half of Holland and part of Alsace, German troops were defending their own borders. It was clear that the Allies were about to launch the final assault.

Hitler decided to attempt a large-scale westward offensive. His army would cross the Ardennes again and heave on towards Antwerp, the centre of Allied food supplies. He hoped to win time and then to turn his main force against the Russians. At the end of December 1944, the German offensive caught the Americans off guard. Flying bombs and rockets (V_1's and V_2's) rained down on Antwerp. By January, however, the German advance had been halted. Again the British and the Americans disagreed about how to proceed. Montgomery repeated his proposal that a concentrated force should cross the northern plain, while Eisenhower preferred not to take the risk and to advance only as far as the Rhine. Since the American force was by far the larger, the Americans were in a position to have their own way. In February 1945 the Colmar pocket fell to the French First Army. The British and the Americans implemented their plan within six weeks, while Hitler repeated the classical error of ordering his troops to resist rather than putting the protection of the Rhine between themselves and the enemy. On 7 March, the Allies luckily captured a bridge intact at Remagen. The die was cast. The principal attack would strike across the centre of Germany. First ten thousand bombers dropped 50,000

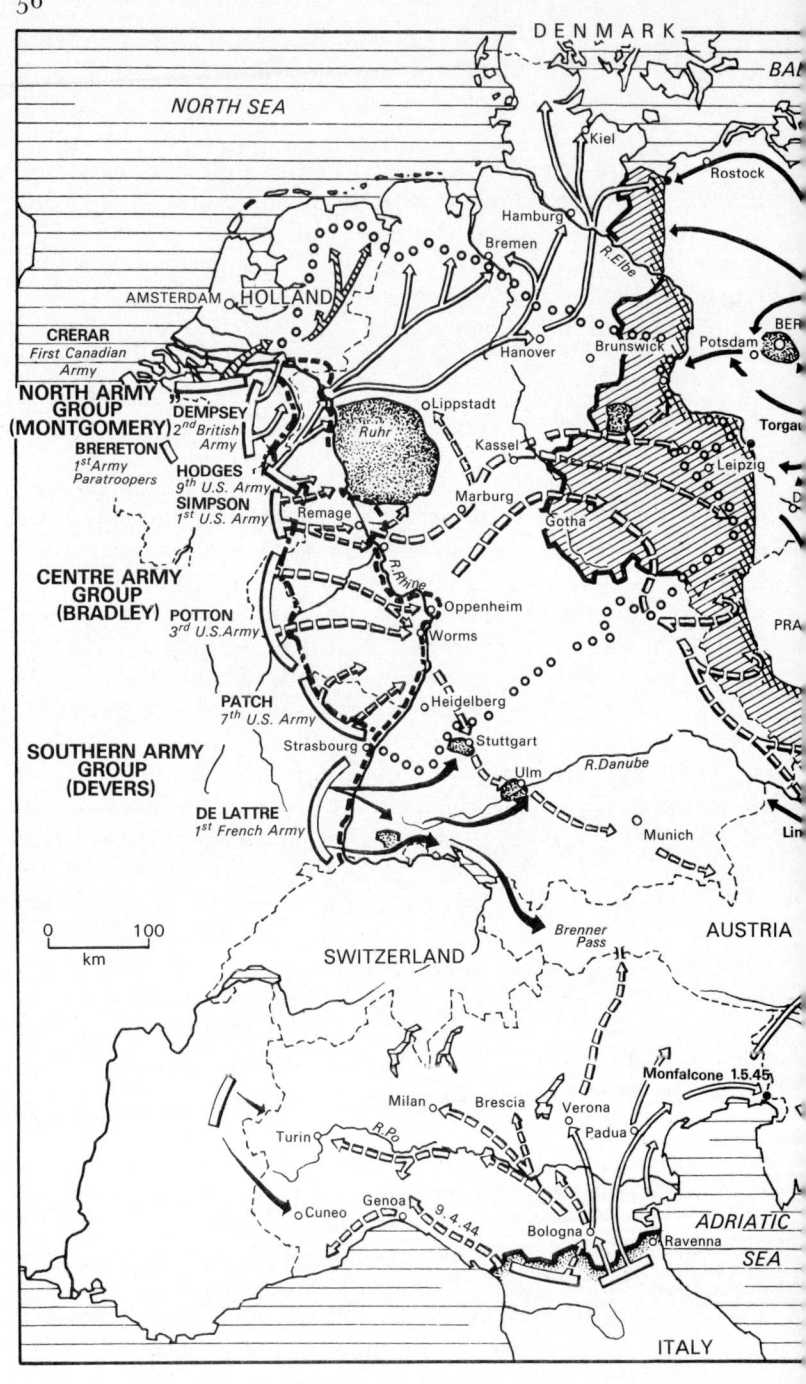

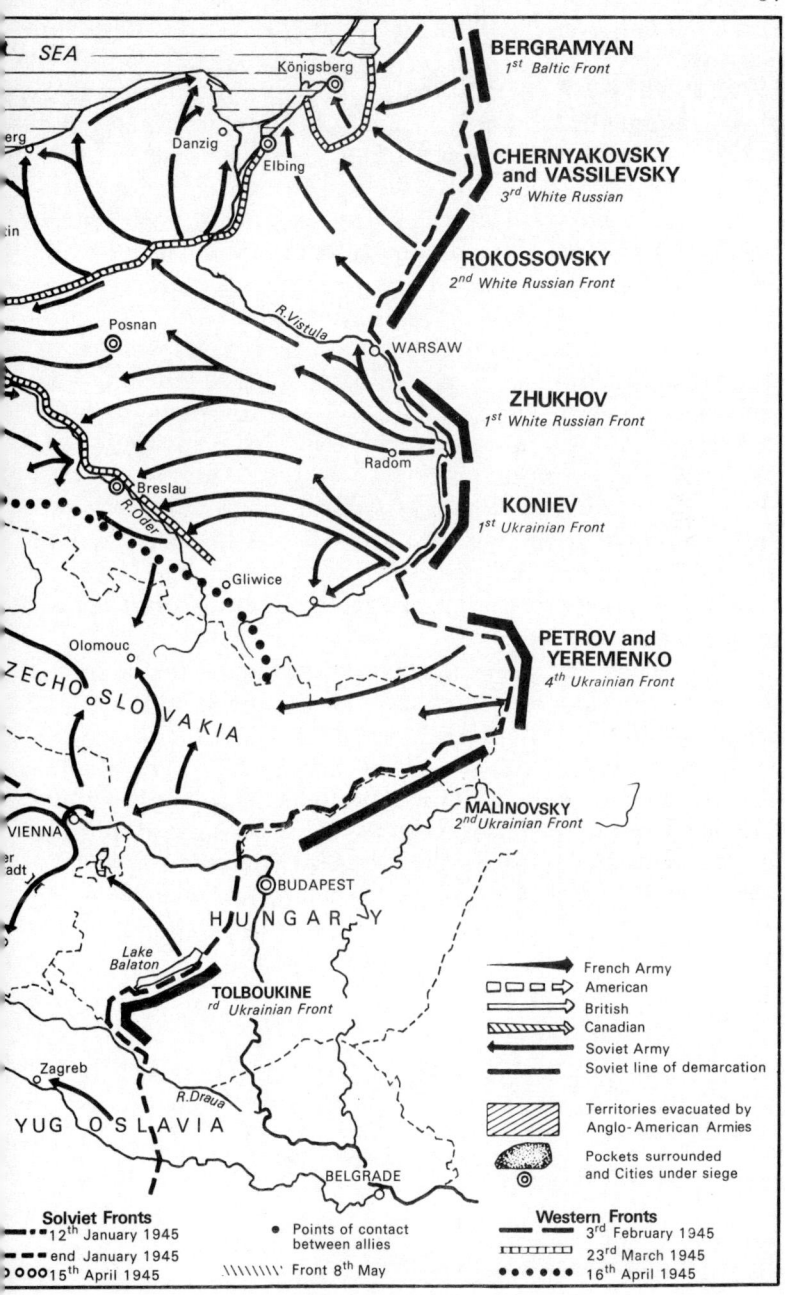

The Final Assault on Germany.

tons of bombs on the Ruhr, which the Allies then began to occupy.

The Russians were held outside Budapest. Although the Germans continued to resist at a number of points on the Baltic coast, where the latest models of the electric submarines were under construction, elsewhere the Red Army continued its advance towards the main target – Berlin. In January it reached the middle Oder between Breslau and Kuestrin. Here it halted while pockets of German resistance were cleared away, particularly at the mouth of the Vistula. In the meantime, it made slow progress across Slovakia, and rapid progress towards Vienna. By the beginning of April 1945, although the Anglo-American army was closer to Berlin, and closer still to Prague than the Red Army, it did not try to reach Berlin first. Churchill alone discerned the political importance of this. After Roosevelt's illness and death, decisions were left to Eisenhower, who was only interested by military problems. His main worry was to link up with the Red Army without exposing either army to attack. He expected a last defensive operation from German strongholds in the Tyrol.

Nazi Germany had begun to disintegrate. One after another, arms factories came to a standstill. Planes and tanks ran out of petrol. Hordes of refugees fled before the Russians. Whole cities had been reduced to rubble and death. Some of Hitler's immediate subordinates, including Himmler, deemed that it was time to surrender to the Western Allies, in the hope of splitting up the 'strange Alliance'. The Germans continued fiercely to resist the Russians, but frequently they surrendered to the

German Submarines

	1940	1941	1942	1943	1944	1945
Total force[a]	58[b]	76	236[c]	405[c]	451	420
In construction	48	195	239	283	234	78[d]
In operation	10 to 12	22 to 91	91[c]	212[c]	168[c]	
Losses	30[b]	35	70	237	236	120[e]

[a] At January 1.
[b] Between September 1939 and December 1940.
[c] Average for the year.
[d] From January to March.
[e] From January to April.

Western Allies. Until the very last moment Hitler counted on new weapons secretly being developed, including the electric submarines, rockets, jet aeroplanes, and perhaps the atomic bomb. But it was too late. Roosevelt's death did not revive the 'miracle of the house of Brandenburg.' In April German defences collapsed in every sector. In Italy, Alexander's troops reached the Po Valley. Vienna fell. The American and Russian forces linked up at Torgau on the Elbe. On 22 April Berlin was surrounded and bombarded by 25,000 heavy guns; it surrendered on 2 May. On 30 April Hitler committed suicide in his bunker 500 yards from the Russian lines. The German army surrendered unconditionally on all fronts, despite the efforts of Admiral Doenitz, Hitler's successor, to delay the defeat. On 7 May at Rheims, Jodl signed Nazi Germany's death certificate in Eisenhower's presence; Keitel in Zhukov's presence the next day at Berlin.

The Defeat and Surrender of Japan

Japan remained. The Americans, who regarded the Far Eastern war as their special preserve, dealt capably with it. Before the fighting in Europe had ended, they had begun to shift troops to the Far East. But they had taken the offensive earlier and had enjoyed a few successes. In China they had met with serious reverses. Roosevelt foresaw that after the war China would play an important part in world affairs. He regarded China as a fourth power. In order to feed the Chinese army by opening the Burma Road, he had accepted a plan for Burma which the British had put up as part of the defence of India. After some fierce fighting Burma was effectively conquered. On 2 May Rangoon fell. All the American advisers, weapons and dollars, however, could not sort out Chiang Kai-Shek's muddled administration in China. The Chinese army remained a hotch-potch of isolated gangs, although in territories under its control it helped the air offensive which the huge B29 bombers unleashed on Japan.

No unified command was set up to handle Pacific operations. Admiral Nimitz and General MacArthur presided over separate campaigns. American organization and method were everywhere admirable. Not only did they quickly make good the losses at Pearl Harbour, they went on to launch twenty large air-

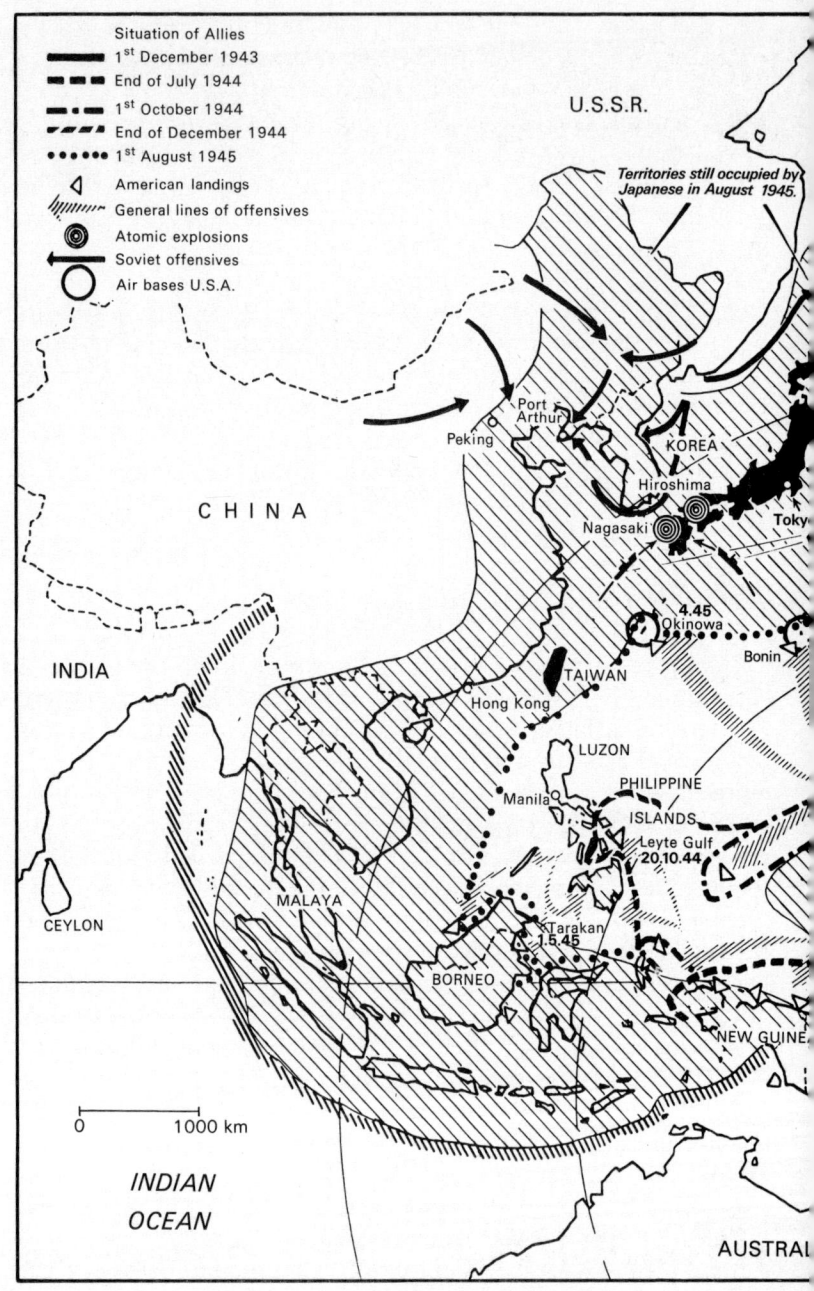

The American Counter-offensive in the Pacific.

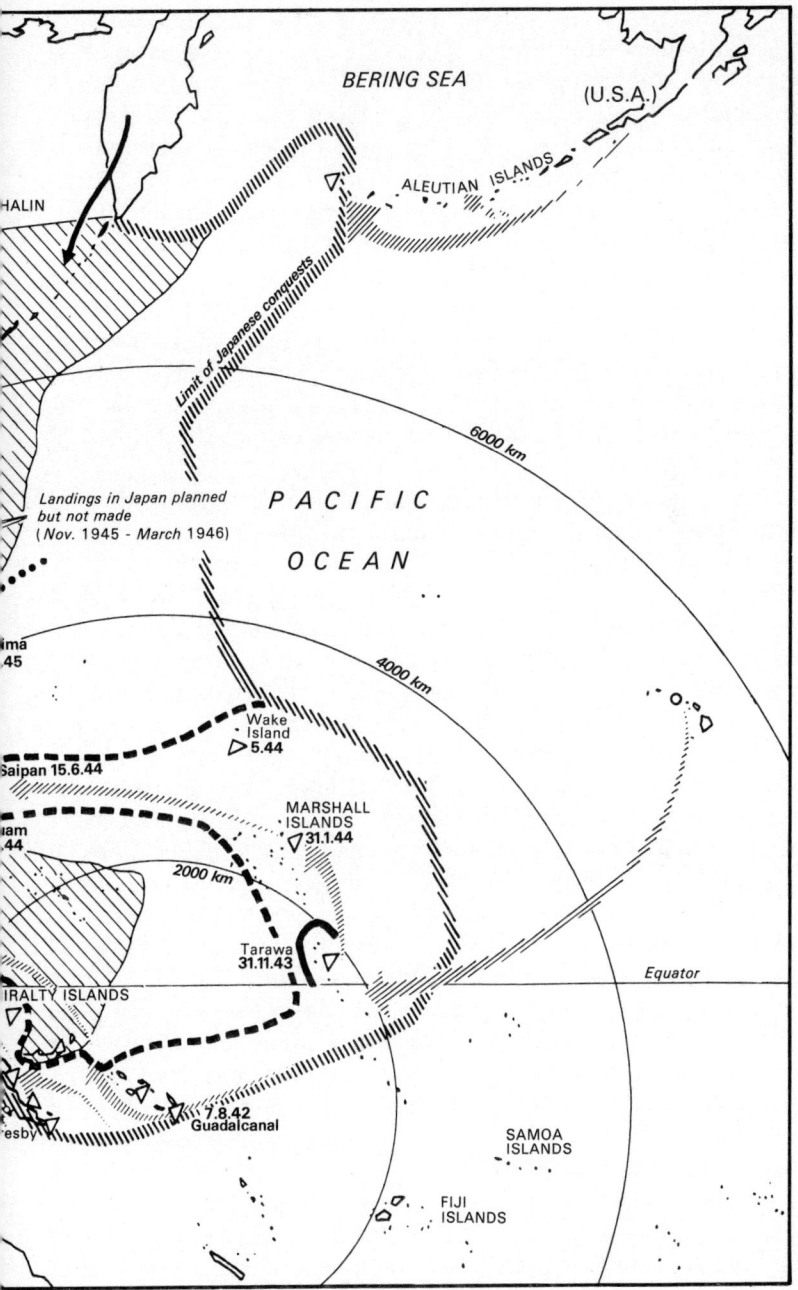

craft carriers, which manoeuvred in close cooperation with the battleships. Their bombers, the B29's were perfectly adapted for long range bombing; they could haul nine tons of bombs a distance of 3500 miles. Men, arms, equipment and food sailed at regular intervals 6,000 miles from the Pacific coast of the United States. American strategists perfected a new landing technique in which special troups, the marines, formed bridge-heads under cover of aerial bombardment and fire from ships off shore. The Japanese could not match American air and sea power. The Japanese fighter planes were slower, their radar and radio installations were less precise. They made up for some of their disadvantage with fierce fighting. They fortified the least atolls and defended them down to the last man. They flew the Kamikaze suicide planes and crashed them into the bridges of enemy ships.

The outcome of the Pacific war hinged on gigantic air and sea battles, which the Japanese frequently lost. The major battles were fought in the Mariana Islands in June 1944, and at Leyte Gulf in October, in both of which the Japanese lost aircraft carriers and battleships. As the Americans increased their control of the sea, they had more freedom of manoeuvre. They disregarded some Japanese strongpoints, which could not be reached by supplies and became prisons for their inhabitants. They landed on others and used them as bases for further advances. Thus the Solomons, New Guinea, the Marianas, the Palaus were successively captured or neutralized, and MacArthur, true to his promise, returned to the Philippines in January 1945. While the Philippine archipelago was being captured, the Americans made two more leaps forward to Iwojima and then to Okinawa, where they were within range of Hondo, the capital island of the Japanese archipelago.

By spring 1945, the Japanese were isolated from their empire. Essential supplies were running short. Japan was shattered by bomb attacks whose devastating effects were increased by gigantic fires. She was on her last legs. By the end of the European war most of her merchant fleet and navy had been lost. Without iron ore, ships and plane manufacture was jeopardized, while the remaining planes and ships had run short of fuel. Nevertheless the Japanese fought so fiercely that the Americans hesitated to land on Hondo. At Okinawa the Japanese lost 110,000 men: only 7,500 were taken prisoners. The Americans reckoned a million men would perish in a landing on Hondo. After this they would still have to defeat the units scattered across the remains of the Japanese Empire. At the Yalta conference Roosevelt had obtained a promise of cooperation from the Red Army in Manchuria, which opened fighting on the eastern front on 9 August with considerable success. But Truman had decided to explode the first atomic bomb at Hiroshima three days earlier. On 9 August another, the last, was dropped on Nagasaki with the same horrific results. The Emperor Hirohito broke his silence to order the last indomitable soldiers to stop fighting. Many of them committed harakiri. The Japanese surrender was signed on 2 September in Tokyo Bay aboard the *Missouri*, an American battleship which had survived Pearl Harbour. The war was over. The Allies had been completely victorious.

V The World at the End of the War

The Conferences at Yalta and Potsdam

Before the fighting had stopped, the Allies had begun to look ahead to the 'post-war.' Each pursued his own interests. Roosevelt's ideas had been summed up in the Atlantic Charter. Although America harboured no secret plans for conquest, the financial and economic boom brought by the war magnified her domination of the American continent at the expense of France and especially Great Britain. Ironically the American President's chief concern as the war was ending was that a third world war should not follow. This was the only event which he imagined could poison a lasting friendship among the Three Great Allies. He devoted all his efforts to preserving this friendship. Stalin had hesitated to accept the Atlantic Charter, but now he did not hesitate to show his hand. Populations which had once been part of Russia were not to be given a chance to oppose annexation. The master of the Kremlin intended to keep all territories acquired under the Russo-German pact. In September 1944 he demanded back the territories which Finland had absorbed with the help of Wehrmacht.

Churchill hammered out two principles of his own. He wanted to prevent any recurrence of a German hegemony over Europe; and he wanted to preserve British power. He did not feel that the provisions of the Atlantic Charter applied to subjects of the British Empire. As for Europe, he may have reckoned that the Red Army would be too exhausted to continue fighting after Soviet Russia had been liberated, but the Red Army's westward advance placed Stalin in a strong negotiating position which Stalin would use to advantage. Churchill flew to Moscow in October 1944 and haggled out a bargain with Stalin, in which a complicated system of percentages was devised to determine who would have how much influence over which territories in central Europe.

In February 1945 at Yalta, and again in July 1945 at Potsdam, the Americans and the British occupied a weak position. At the meeting in the Crimea, they were just recovering from the German attack on the Ardennes. At both meetings their chief aim was to enlist the Russians' help against Japan. At Potsdam Truman, who succeeded Roosevelt, knew that he could rely on the atom bomb, but no one knew what effect it would have on the war. Signs of conflict between Soviet Russia and Great Britain worried Roosevelt, though he hoped to keep America out of it. Regardless of later accusations that Roosevelt conceded too much to Stalin, he actually did make an effort to avoid nettling him. For all Truman's suspicions and obstinacy, he struck much the same conciliatory tone at Potsdam. The Anglo-Americans agreed to withdraw their forces from the zone occupied by the Russians in Germany, even though Churchill would have preferred to leave them there as a bargaining point in later negotiations with Stalin, but Churchill was forced to yield. Britain was no longer a front-rank power. The Labour Party swept Churchill out of power in the parliamentary elections which followed victory in Europe. His successor, Clement Attlee was not as great a man as Churchill. He took a keener interest in internal British affairs, than in negotiations with Russia and America, in which he played the role of the outsider. The Yalta conference did not carve up the world, as everyone has said and written since, but it did create a form of joint governance, later affirmed at Potsdam, by which the two super-powers thrown up by the war would regulate world affairs. Together they settled a number of questions which had been left in abeyance – the occupation and administration of Germany, the Polish question, the status of the central European countries which had been satellites of the Reich, the future of the colonial empires, the occupation and administration of Japan, the creation and organization of a new League of Nations. Other minor issues were also settled, such as rights of access through the Turkish straits, the status of Tangiers, the evacuation of Iran, the occupation of Austria, and freedom of navigation in international waterways.

The Fate of Germany

The Allies did not disagree about Germany. Since 1944 it had been decided that Germany would be completely occupied. Each of the Allied armies was to occupy its own zone within definite borders. At Yalta Churchill had argued that France could have a balancing effect on Europe if she were rearmed. Roosevelt readily, and Stalin more reluctantly, accepted France as a fourth occupying power. A French zone was chiselled out of the existing British and American Zones. Each of the four occupying forces would also control a sector of Berlin, which lay within the Russian zone. The four military commanders would administer common affairs jointly. Roosevelt imagined this complicated scheme would serve as a forced contract to preserve good relations among the Allies. A permanent dismemberment of Germany had been mooted several times and Stalin had always assented. At Potsdam he mysteriously reversed his opinion. The question was dropped. Only France held out for the creation of an autonomous Rhineland state.

The Allies were adamant that Nazi crimes should be punished. The responsible people would be tried at an International Military Tribunal at Nuremberg, the former Mecca of Nazism. A huge sum was allotted for German war reparations; negotiations had started on the basis of Stalin's figure of $20,000 million, of which Soviet Russia would receive half. She would recover it from the other zones as well as from her own zone. Germany would be disarmed so as to prevent renewed agression. Her 'excessive' economic power would be attenuated, and her institutions and her national character would be denazified. Military police would supervise a gradual reinstatement of rights and privileges, but no central administration would be reestablished. General de Gaulle was particularly firm on this point. The German people were ruined. They were condemned as a single mass, their lives reduced to chaos. Only Churchill was concerned with how they would feed themselves or produce enough to live on and pay reparations.

The Polish Question

From Teheran onwards the fate of Poland was interwoven with that of the Reich. Only another war could have prevented Stalin from reabsorbing Poland's eastern provinces, which were populated by Bielorussians and Ukrainans. No one wanted to gamble on a war between the Allies. The solution was to repay Poland with the territory from the west up to the Oder Neisse line. The Polish government in London and the Lublin Committee concurred on this one point. Stalin wanted this adjustment of the Western frontier to produce a permanent amalgamation of Poland with Germany. Only Churchill had qualms about 'stuffing the Polish goose'. However, there was an Eastern Neisse and a Western Neisse. At Yalta, a final choice between the two was postponed until a peace treaty had been drawn up. At Potsdam Soviet Russia confronted her allies with two accomplished facts: direct rule had been restored within the territories which in principle belonged to Poland; and the western frontiers of these territories coincided with the Eastern Neisse. Since the German population had largely withdrawn from the area and Polish settlers had begun to replace them, the question had been settled in practice if not by law.

The British and Americans had advocated joint rule in Poland by the London and Lublin governments, but Stalin regarded the London government as enemies of Russia and refused it status equal with Lublin. The Lublin Committee had already established itself in Poland and was making laws and administering them. The London rivals were interned. Stalin called a meeting of the Polish resistance leaders at Moscow and threw them into prison. The Americans and British had no choice but to give in. As the skeleton of the new Polish government was communist, it was clear that Poland would adjust her internal and foreign policies to accord with Soviet Russia. It was agreed that the Polish people should have the opportunity of ratifying the arrangement in a free election, but when it came to the fact, Stalin vigorously opposed the presence of foreign observers in Poland during the elections. He argued that this would be an insult to the Poles. The elections were supervised by the Red Army.

Central Europe

Stalin's behaviour shocked Churchill and Roosevelt. They each had a different concept of democracy. Soviet Russia was assembling a new kind of empire cemented by ideology. The government of each country would orientate itself towards the Russian camp either willingly or by constraint. Communists, usually heads of the communist parties returning from Moscow, became members of National Union governments. The 'fascists' and their supporters were immediately prosecuted. This formula was adopted without objection by the Bulgarians, who had not opposed Soviet Russia in the War, and had always been on friendly terms with the Russians.

In Rumania the national front was splintered by the communist policy of reapportionment of land and nationalization of industry. In February 1945 Vychinski, the Soviet Vice-Minister of Foreign Affairs, arrived at Bucarest and issued King Michael an ultimatum to change the government in accordance with Soviet policies and to appoint a communist as minister of the interior. Roosevelt and Churchill proposed setting up a tripartite commission, but Stalin politely refused. In Czechoslovakia, Benes agreed to appoint a communist head of government. Rumania and Czechoslovakia had both been strongly pro-Western.

In Hungary the communists tried unsuccessfully to seize power. They were a minority party within the liberation committee which had been set up at Debreczen. The Red Army treated Hungary as an enemy and occupied it on the grounds that it had been a long standing German ally. In Yugoslavia the communists were completely successful. Tito formed a National Council government in March 1945. He himself was head of the government and partisans filled 23 of the 28 ministerial posts. Under the agreement between Stalin and Churchill influence was to have been shared equally between them. In the final event Churchill was very bitter. He felt he had been duped. At the time it was not known that Stalin and Tito did not see eye to eye. All the central European states had entered the Russian sphere irrespective of their wartime policies. Only Greece escaped. Churchill had been adamant and Stalin upheld his part of the bargain. But Greece was soon rent by civil war, possibly at Russia's provocation, and the outcome seemed uncertain.

The Colonial Empires

By being defeated, the conquered nations lost their colonial empires. France proposed that Italy should retain her territories under mandate. Molotov claimed part of Tripolitania for Soviet Russia 'so that she would occupy her rightful place in the Mediterranean.' But at a meeting at London in September 1945 the Allies decided to grant independence to Ethiopia, Libya and Somaliland. The British expected all three new states to gather beneath her protective wing. Japan returned Formosa and Manchuria to China and Port Arthur and northern Sakhalin to Soviet Russia. The Koreans regained their independence.

Victory did not spare the Allies' empires, where their armies had too often been discredited. America under Roosevelt's leadership repeatedly remonstrated against colonialism. Nationalist leaders were aware that the colonizers themselves were in disagreement. During the war the Allies renounced their 'territorial concessions' and privileges in China. As soon as Japan had been defeated, Sukarno claimed independence for Indonesia. The Dutch could not restore their administration without reconquering the Indonesian empire. The French Empire, particularly in Africa, remained loyal during the war, but French authority had been undermined by the presence of the English in the Middle East and Madagascar, by the Americans in French North Africa, and by the Japanese in Indochina. The Middle Eastern countries had to be granted independence. On the day the Germans surrendered an uprising broke out at Sétif in Algeria, which had to be put down with bloodshed. After the Japanese withdrew from Indochina, the Chinese occupied it in the north and Great Britain in the south. Viet-Minh nationalists infiltrated everywhere. The outlook was grim. The British Empire seemed to emerge from the war unscathed, but Canada and Australia had shifted a little further away from Britain towards American influence. During the war Burma had been promised independence. As the war ended, India was lashed by strikes, popular uprisings and mutinies.

The Fate of Japan

The Americans regarded the future of Japan as their own concern. In 1942 they had begun to study the problems posed by occupation and what powers should be granted to the military command. After some hesitation, they decided not to depose the Emperor. He retained his title, disendowed of divine powers, and served as mediator to make the Japanese more receptive of

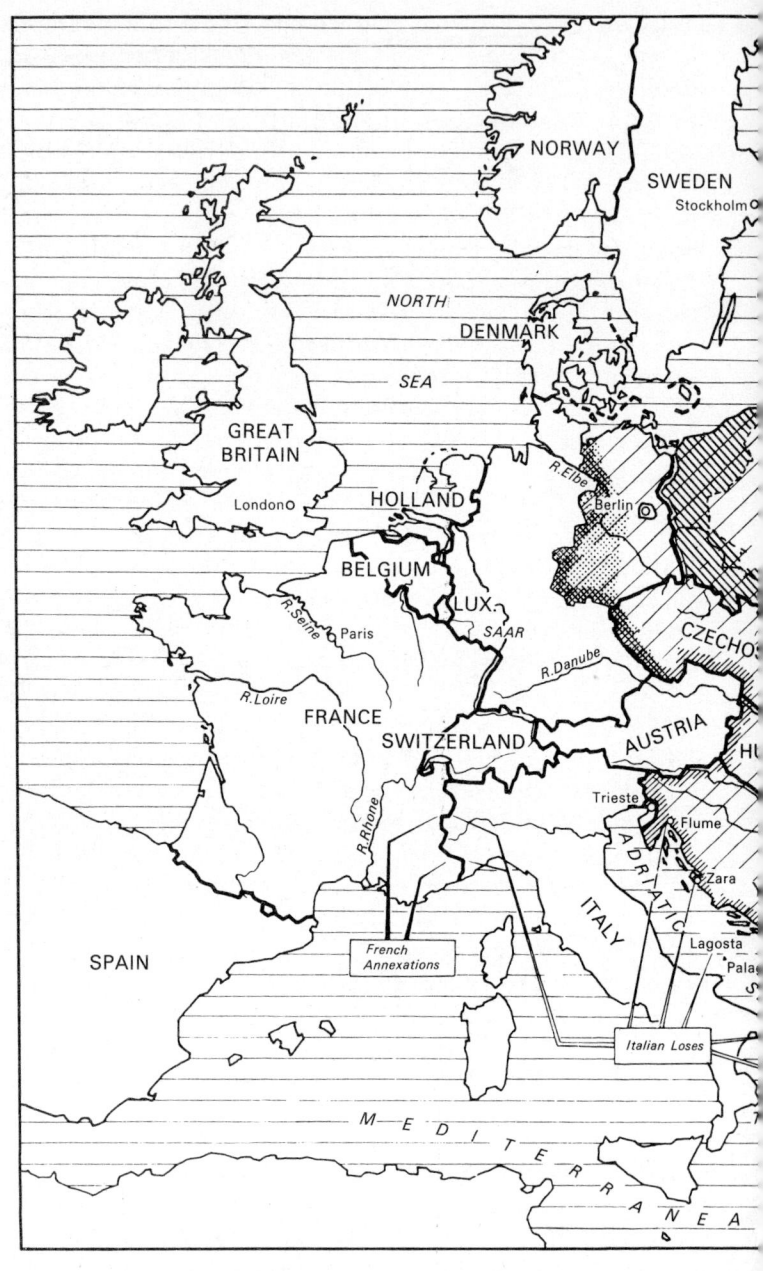

Europe at the end of the war.

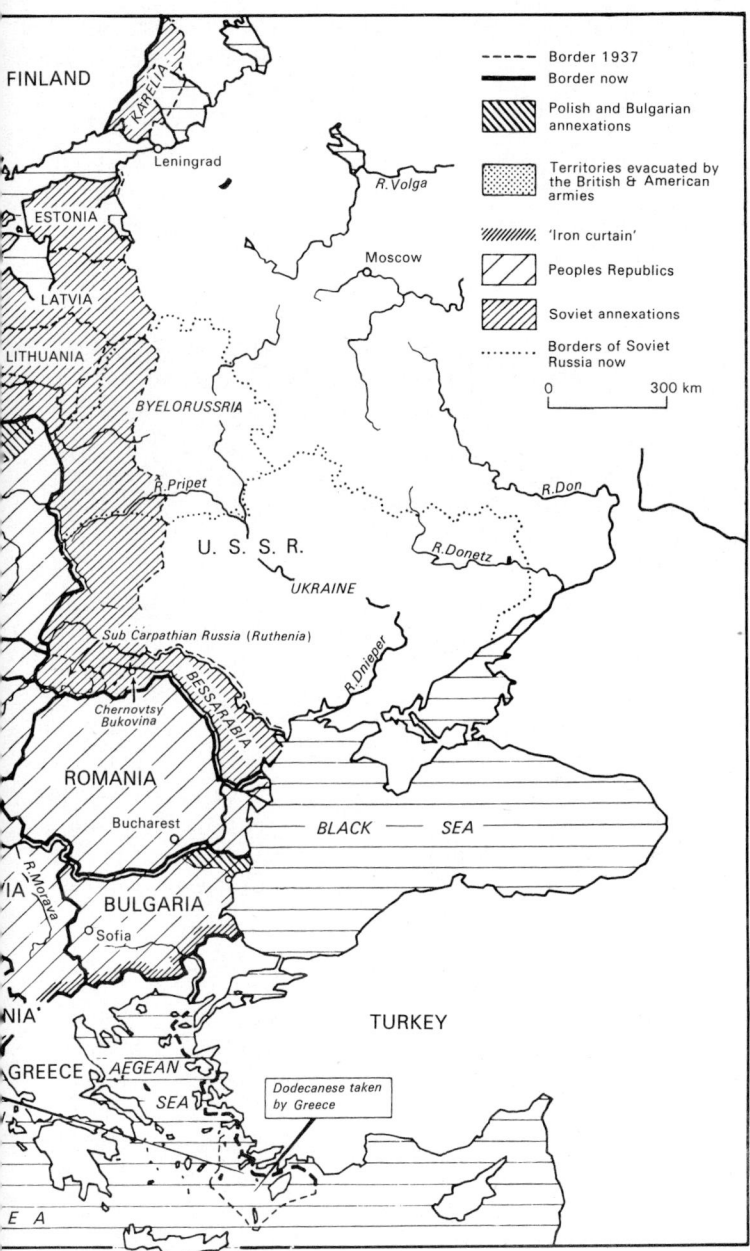

American policy. Representatives of all the allied countries attended the surrender ceremony and served on the occupation commission in a consultative capacity. At Tokyo war criminals were tried and sentenced by a tribunal. At General MacArthur's order, as supreme commander for the Allied Powers, Japan was demilitarized and democratized.

The United Nations Organization

The Allies settled all the questions which the end of the war had posed without breaking off relations, though not without increasingly bitter feelings. Unlike the winning nations in the First World War, they assigned the task of keeping the peace in future to a new League of Nations, which, unlike the old one, did not owe its existence to a peace treaty. Roosevelt was the chief architect.

In January 1942 the Department of State drafted a United Nations Declaration. Under it the powers fighting against the Axis would undertake to remain united after the war. Soviet Russia signalled her assent at Teheran, and a study group was formed at Washington. In September 1944, the Four Great Powers – the United States, Soviet Russia, Great Britain and China, but not France – met again at Dumbarton Oaks in America to settle the general outline of the United Nations Organization. It would comprise two central institutions, a General Assembly and a Security Council, in which the Five Great Allies (including France) would be permanent members. The proposals were finally adopted at the Yalta Conference. Stalin and Churchill did not envisage the same future for the United Nations as Roosevelt. Stalin's primary concern was to ensure against a resurgence of German imperialism. Churchill wanted to preserve British power. Both wanted to carve up the world into spheres of influence. Roosevelt disagreed. He maintained that international relations should be ruled by international law; the powerful should respect the rights and the autonomy of the weak. It was agreed that all the states which had fought in the Allied camp would become members of the General Assembly on equal footing. The English secured places for their dominions and Soviet Russia created places for Bielorussia and the Ukraine. Although the New United Nations was to be granted greater scope for independent action than the old League of Nations, the notion of creating a super-state to which the members would delegate part of their sovereignty was not considered.[16] Peace would last only as long as the Great Powers wanted. Responsibility for keeping peace was given to the Security Council; but since its decisions had to be unanimous, it was condemned to impotence whenever one of the Great Powers deemed its special interests to be at stake.

The United Nations convened at San Francisco between 25 April and 25 June 1945. A number of other international institutions which had been set up to deal with specific problems during the war were preserved. The U.N.R.R.A. (the United Nations Relief and Rehabilitation Agency) was set up in February 1943 to distribute food supplies to countries impoverished by the war. The International Labour Organization was set up in October 1944. The International Bank for Reconstruction and Development and the International Monetary Fund were founded at Bretton Woods in July 1944. UNESCO (United Nations Education, Science and Culture Organization) was founded at London in 1943.

Losses and Destruction

While the war was still wreaking immense destruction the Allies pondered the immense problem of repairing the damage afterwards. The death toll and material losses were staggering. There are no exact figures, but a reasonable estimate would be that 50 million lives were lost, about four times as many as in the First World War. Half of them were civilians. Twenty million Russians perished, ten per cent of the population. In Poland fifteen per cent of the population were killed. The Germans lost five million, three quarters of them on the eastern front, and half a million in the bombing. In western Europe the losses were smaller, but as many died from Nazi crimes as in combat – another peculiar feature of this war. As there was no civil government in China, no exact figures are calculable but losses must have been between three and eight million. It is estimated that the genocide against the Jews claimed six million lives. The Americans, who fought on both fronts, lost only 300,000 soldiers, but they had had to finance the equipment used in the war by their allies and partners. The death of 200,000 people in a few seconds at Hiroshima and Nagasaki revealed how great the toll a new war might bring.

The military operations resulted in several large migrations of populations from Lorraine and Poland and the exchanges of populations in the Tyrol, while others were caused by fear, such as the exodus of June 1940 in France and the retreat of a million Germans before the advancing Red Army in 1945. In addition, there were millions of prisoners of war. In Germany, prisoners of war, conscripts in the compulsory labour forces and internees in concentration camps amounted to nearly fifteen million. But no country was spared. Workers withdrew across the Urals in Soviet Russia and they migrated from the rural South to the industrial North East in America. There were about 30 million displaced persons in all. Several years after the end of the war, a million were still interned in temporary camps without anywhere to settle.

Material destruction was also gigantic, particularly because fighting occurred over wide areas and because both camps advanced and retreated over the same territories but also because bombardments from the air and from the ground forces were heavy and because reprisal operations were often devastating. Germany, Soviet Russia, and Poland were most affected. A Polish report estimated that 80 per cent of transport facilities, 50 per cent of agricultural livestock, and 31 per cent of the national product were lost in the war. In Yugoslavia 20 per cent of houses were destroyed. In France about 55,000 miles of railways were destroyed and 24,000 miles were damaged; 1900 works of art were destroyed. Most cities in Germany and Japan were reduced to rubble. Italy was ravaged from south to north, but the richest region in the Po Valley escaped serious destruction. Great Britain, too, did not escape. Only the United States emerged from the war without the least material loss. But the blind destruction of cities and works of art, attacks on civilians, above all the Nazi crimes, in which scientists themselves were accomplices, inflicted moral wounds, especially in Europe, which were deeper and more difficult to repair than damage to property.

Once again, the cost of the war was infinitely greater than the problems which caused it. In a sense, the war did answer some questions. The Allies did fulfil their aims and their victory did restore collective and individual freedom in the occupied states. The Allies had fought to preserve justice and law. The discovery of Nazi atrocities demonstrated that these were not merely propaganda slogans. But the war arose out of political instability and it created new forms of instability.

Europe

Europe was especially weakened by the war. Several front-rank powers of 1939 had slipped to second rank by 1945, not only countries which had lost the war but also some that had won. Italy, which had changed camps early enough to avoid disaster, emerged in generally passable form, with the loss of a few small parts of Istria and some French Alps, which did not seriously damage her territorial integrity. But the war revealed serious flaws in her economic structure. Democracy was restored too quickly and some fascist elements survived. It was only the common opposition to fascism which had united the various factions of the resistance movement. Initially the Italians relied on aid from the British and Americans to set their economy going and to distribute food to the populations.

In Germany, catastrophe was absolute. By 1945, there was nothing left. Rarely had such exuberant expansion been succeeded so rapidly by such overwhelming defeat. Industrial equipment, railways and roads were wrecked. The Russians set the seal on the destruction by carrying off what functional machines remained. The state had been wiped out; Germany had ceased to exist. Only the Germans remained, demoralized by their losses, by the absence of 3 million prisoners of war, by the infamy of the Nazi crimes, by their implacable conquerers who were eager for revenge. The exodus from the east overcrowded the west. In the British zone population density rose to 246 per square kilometer. Moral standards lapsed. There was threat of famine. Unemployment was nearly universal. On the other hand, the disappearance of the class of great landowners and Prussian officers transformed society. The mines were intact and some sectors of industry were not as severely disabled as others. But bankruptcy could not end and recovery could not begin without the Allies' consent. Only the Americans showed concern. In the meanwhile, a great vacuum had formed in central Europe.

France could not fill it, although she was one of the conquerors. She had reorientated herself with impressive speed. The resistance fostered a new spirit which united popular opinion briefly behind the noble figure of General de Gaulle. With moderate state control, France turned over a new economic leaf, but she had to struggle with some serious shortages and she was harassed by inflation. General de Gaulle's foreign policy was ambitious. He wanted to turn the Rhineland into a French dependency. He tried to form an alliance with Soviet Russia in order to counterbalance British and American domination, but the Three Great Powers did not regard France as an equal. Her reconstruction was financed by American aid.

Great Britain's position was similar. History teaches disappointing lessons. Britain, which had held out against Germany without losing heart in the most discouraging days of the war and to which the free world owed a huge debt, was reduced to a state of near-servitude. The Royal Navy had been surpassed by the American Navy, Britain had lost 6 million tons of merchant shipping between 1939 and 1945, and her merchant fleet was now barely a third the size of America's. London's financial markets were no longer the most important in the world. Huge investments had been lost in South America, and large sums were owed to the Dominions. The bills incurred under Lend-Lease were cancelled, but Britain was still forced to negotiate a loan from the United States repayable over fifty years. Workers clamoured for social reforms. They had contributed to the war effort without complaining and the Labour Government could no longer put them off. The effort to maintain full employment, to nationalize key industries and to carry out the Beveridge Plan could not be reconciled with a prestigious role in world affairs. The Empire began to dissolve, and the Labour Party were not reluctant to be rid of it.

Asia

Asia was left in an unsettled state. The Japanese empire disappeared leaving nothing in its place. The damage to industry, the destruction of Japanese merchant and military fleets, and the deaths of so many citizens left the Japanese economy in serious straits. The population was demoralized. Their myths and beliefs had been discredited. Their attempt to preserve their culture while assimilating Western technology seemed to have miscarried. They submitted blindly to the American occupation without knowing what it would bring.

China was among the winners, but her condition was little better. After the Japanese withdrew, the internecine conflict between the Kuomintang faction and the communists flared up again. India was near independence, but it was also divided between Hindus of the Congress Party and the Muslims of the League. British presence had warded away civil strife and withdrawal seemed certain to bring partition and bloodshed. Indochina and Indonesia were in turmoil. The war never stopped. The defeat of the colonizers undermined the artificial unity created by their presence. The attack on Pearl Harbour had forced the Americans to settle in most of the Pacific Islands, where they remained after the war.

Soviet Russia

Two super-powers, Soviet Russia and America, emerged from the havoc. They were not evenly matched. Soviet Russia had dispelled doubts about the survival of her army, her industry, her population, and above all her political and social system. For a long time during the course of the war she had borne the full weight of the enemy on her own. She was compensated by two kinds of expansion. She was the only one of the Great Allies to gain in this way from the war. On the one hand she annexed the Karelian Isthmus from Finland, the Baltic states, Lithuania, the formerly Polish sections of Bielorussia and the Ukraine, Ruthenia from Czechoslovakia, Bessarabia and North Bukovina from Rumania, Koenigsberg and East Prussia, the Kurile Islands, the southern part of Sakhalin, the port of Dairen and Port Arthur. On the other hand, she had acquired new allies with the help of her army and of local communist parties. In Europe her influence extended up to the Elbe and Vienna, in Asia to Manchuria and North Korea and Northern Iran. She would have a say in the administration of the Ruhr. She would be present at Tokyo and at Tangiers. Her losses in men and materials, however, overwearied and impoverished her, and recovery would be slow and difficult. The war had revealed weaknesses in transport and in the production of consumer goods, though production had dramatically increased in the Urals and beyond. For a long time the Red Army remained the only large army in Europe, and victory brought immense prestige. Stalin's 'deviations', his 'purges', and 'trials', and his pact with Germany were forgotten.

The Russians espoused pan-slavism and orthodoxy, and availed themselves of their own Muslim population to gain a foothold in the Arab world. The rule of expediency enhanced Russia's status as capital of international communism, despite the suppression of Comintern. Communism prevailed throughout central and eastern Europe and gained strength in France and Italy. In the war Soviet Russia learned how to blend revolutionary impulse with nationalism, and how to make use of the mixture which they produced.

The United States

As soon as the Germans surrendered, Truman cut off Lend-Lease to Russia. Stalin's protests revealed the fundamental difference in actual power between the two countries. The American giant overflowed with prosperity and optimism. The population had grown in the war despite the death toll and the mobilization of millions of men. Full employment had been achieved. National income had doubled in five years and the national budget was balanced, although national debt had quadrupled. Production had advanced in every sector, 33 per cent in agriculture, 40 per cent in petroleum, 400 per cent in iron ore. Ninty-five million tons of steel left the furnaces. The shipyards were launching two times as many ships each year as were sunk by the German submarines during the worst days of the Battle of the Atlantic. America had become the largest naval power in the world, and she had almost a monopoly on intercontinental air navigation.

By the end of the war 60 per cent of the world's gold reserves were lodged in the reserve banks of the United States, and the dollar was the only gold-based currency left. Although commercial overproduction yielded large surpluses, and profits were large, wealth was unevenly distributed. Workers' standard of living had improved, but they objected to huge profits distributed by many businesses. Some regions, the South in particular, were slightly poorer at the end of the war. Some sectors of the population – Blacks, Puerto Ricans, Mexicans, and the French Canadians – were relatively deprived and underdeveloped.

The American influence prevailed throughout the world. Everyone owed America something. Canada and South America were completely under her power, although South America did not adjust easily to the American way of life, which benefited only a privileged minority of the population. At the end of the war, many soldiers returned with the idea that an era had ended, that America would turn her back on the world and settle down again to isolationist indifference. Her leaders, including President Truman, were uncertain how to proceed, but America was now too large a power to escape heavy foreign commitments. She still had to come to terms with this. The end of the war marked the rise of a new form of American involvement, in Asia especially, as well as in Europe.

The Age of Science and Technology

Wars may pose more problems than they solve. The Allied victory did put down fascist imperialism. Had fascism prospered, society would have evolved in an entirely different way, particularly outside Europe. It is often said that wars interrupt development, which then afterwards continues. But the Second World War seems to have wrought deep and lasting changes which marked a turning point and the opening of a new era. Ironically, while the war was spreading destruction, means were being discovered and developed to repair the damage quickly. Between 1939 and 1945 practical and theoretical research in science advanced in leaps and bounds. One may reasonably record the emergence of a scientific and technological civilization.

A few examples of the technological advances devised or developed during the war were radar, transistors, computers, plastics, DDT, sulphanimides, penicillin, methods of blood transfusion and resuscitation and industrial automation. The grimmest and also the most promising was the technique of harnessing nuclear energy, of which America took the lion's share of the benefits. Progress here was made possible by unwonted facilities granted researchers by governments. A prime example was the cooperative effort organized in America to develop the atomic bomb. Scientific research and technology ceased to be cottage industries and became team work enshrined as activities of national importance. They soon emerged from the laboratory into industry where they were used in the mass application of new methods to improve the output of countless products.

The world after the war was riddled with contradictions. The possibility of creating material wealth had become infinite, but the poor were poorer than ever before. Although distances were reduced and speed brought nations nearer, nations retreated into gloomy nationalism. New methods were available to disseminate knowledge and culture, but whole continents still stagnated in intellectual impassivity. Mobilization and unification of populations in the war effort brought greater uniformity. Everyone was caught up in a whirlwind of scientific progress and its practical applications, but they had yet to master the new technology.

Notes

[1] For a more detailed account, see our *La Seconde Guerre Mondiale*, in the collection Peuples et Civilisations, Presses Universitaires de France (1968–1969), II, 506–540.

[2] A popular slogan quipped. 'We shall win because we are stranger'.

[3] After Mussolini's fall, he added the Northern Tyrol, for which a transfer of population was already half-complete.

[4] Not to mention the German emigrants who had left Europe – in order to go to the United States and Brazil, for example.

[5] During an interview with Hendaye in October 1940, Franco was asked to declare war on Hitler's behalf, but he demanded so much material assistance and so many territorial concessions (Gibraltar, Morocco, Oran, Roussillon) that Hitler did not press the point.

[6] France paid 400 million francs a day, which would have been enough to maintain 10 million soldiers.

[7] Most notably in the influence it allowed the leaders of the Church, and by the absence of a single-party system.

[8] *Schutzstaffel der Nationalsozialitischen Arbeitspartei*, the state security service.

[9] The Japanese also practised racism against American, Dutch and French prisoners of war, particularly against French and Dutch civilians. They were interned in hard conditions, deprived of food and medical attention, defenceless against epidemics. Large numbers died.

[10] For a study of the whole of the resistance, we refer to our work *La Guerre de l'ombre*, Grasset, 1970.

[11] A general survey of the resistance throughout Europe is given in Henri Michel, *La Guerre de l'ombre*, Grasset, 1970.

[12] See our *Histoire de la résistance en France* and *Les courants de pensée de la résistance*, Presses Universitaires de France; also *Jean Moulin l'unificateur*, Hachette, 1970.

[13] A notable exploit of the Czech resistance involved the execution of Heydrich, the 'protector', head of the special services of the Nazi Party. Agents were dropped by parachute from London.

[14] Soviet Russia feared that German invasion would provoke a similar movement. Stalin relocated 300,000 Crimean Tartars to central Asia. The Germans recruited auxiliary forces from racial minorities.

[15] See next chapter.

[16] Except Blum in *A l'échelle humaine*.